Llewellyn's

2021
Witches'
Companion

A Guide to Contemporary Living

D1372727

Llewellyn Publications is a registered trademark of Llewellyn Worldwide Ltd.

Art Director: Lynne Menturweck
Cover art © Tim Foley
Cover designer: Lynne Menturweck

Interior illustrations:
Tim Foley: 9, 34, 71, 79, 102, 129, 151, 193, 197, 235
Bri Hermanson: 23, 42, 112, 142, 182, 227
Rik Olson: 54, 86, 120, 160, 211, 249
M. Kathryn Thompson: 11, 65, 97, 133, 175, 216

ISBN 978-0-7387-5489-5

Llewellyn Worldwide Ltd. does not participate in, endorse, or have any authority or responsibility concerning private business transactions between our authors and the public.

Any internet references contained in this work are current at publication time, but the publisher cannot guarantee that a specific location will continue to be maintained. Please refer to the publisher's website for links to authors' websites and other sources.

You can order Llewellyn annuals and books from *New Worlds*, Llewellyn's magazine catalog. To request a free copy of the catalog, call toll-free 1-877-NEW-WRLD or visit our website at www.llewellyn.com.

Llewellyn Publications
A Division of Llewellyn Worldwide Ltd.
2143 Wooddale Drive
Woodbury, MN 55125-2989
www.llewellyn.com

Printed in the United States of America

Contents

Community Forum

Provocative Opinions on Contemporary Topics

Magical Self-Care

Nurture Your Body, Mind & Spirit

Witchy Living

Day-by-Day Witchcraft

Witchcraft Essentials

Practices, Rituals & Spells

Visiting sacred sites can provide amazing magical experiences that will inspire your practice and invigorate your spirit. However, these experiences can also be frustrating, exhausting, expensive, and even dangerous without proper planning. Here is some practical advice to aid you on your journeys.

The Lunar Calendar

September 2020 to December 2021

Community Forum

PROVOCATIVE OPINIONS ON
CONTEMPORARY TOPICS

Loving Nature to Death: Better Pagan Practices for Your Ecosystem

Lupa

Many pagans would describe themselves as nature-based in their path, enjoying hiking, camping, and other outdoor activities. Common pagan imagery includes animals, plants, fungi, and other living beings, as well as the four physical elements, celestial bodies, and many other natural phenomena.

Yet we still fall prey to practices that do more harm than good to the natural world. We also play our own part in climate change, habitat loss, and other major ecological disasters. And many of the practices common in paganism are directly harmful. Here are some ways to make your practice more eco-friendly.

Safely Dispose of Offerings

This is probably the biggest way that pagans have a tendency to inadvertently do damage with good intentions. Just as with garbage, though, there is no "going away" for things we leave outside, such as offerings or spell components.

Don't leave food offerings out where wildlife can eat them. A lot of the things we like to eat are bad for the wildlife and can make them sick. Wildlife might also not get a complete amount of nutrients from our food; ducks that are fed bread don't eat the natural foods they're supposed to have, leading to serious wing deformities and other conditions.

You're also encouraging wildlife to associate humans with food. They lose their fear of humans, which leads to animals getting hit by cars or having to be shot because they got too aggressive in begging for food. When you artificially increase the amount of food available, you are also directly promoting overpopulation, starvation, and disease.

Do keep food offerings away from wildlife. Eat them yourself or give the food to someone in need. Donate money to a wildlife rehabilitation center so they can buy the sorts of foods their animals need. Plant a variety of native plants that offer wildlife food and shelter year-round. (Wild songbirds and hummingbirds are the one exception to the "don't feed wildlife" rule. These animals are less likely to lose their fear of humans, and bird feeders offset the effects of habitat loss. Never encourage birds to do things like eat out of your hand!)

Don't discard spell bottles, charms, and other non-biodegradable magical items by throwing them into water, tying them to trees, or burying them. Wildlife may eat litter, choke on it, die from a painful intestinal blockage, or slowly starve to death because their stomachs are so full of plastic and trash that they can't eat and digest food. Items tied to tree branches can entangle wildlife and harm or kill the tree. Plastic infests the entire planet, and glass can break and become hazardous to living beings.

Do find better options for your spells that don't involve throwing things away. Make use of items already in nature, such as stones, grass, or legal feathers. If you have to do something destructive, like burning a piece of paper, keep it small. Use non-physical spell aids, like visualizing your intent flying away on the wind or asking a spirit to carry it for you.

Humane Harvesting and Responsible Foraging

Don't pick all of a particular plant or fungus in a given area. Take no more than 25 percent of what you see, unless there are only very few individuals there. In the case of delicate plants such as trillium, picking the flower or leaves can kill the entire plant. Others, like ghost pipe, grow only every few years in a given area and are best left alone.

Do be a responsible forager. Educate yourself on native plants and which ones are at the greatest risk. Ask other pagans, wildcrafters, and foragers about how to ethically forage in your area.

Don't deliberately introduce a non-native species to a place just so you can harvest it. It's one thing if it's your personal garden where you can keep things contained. It's another to go out into a wild area and seed it with non-native herbs or wildflowers. This also goes for fungi; inoculating a dead tree with a non-native fungus can lead to ecological chaos down the road as it spreads from that first host tree.

Do promote the growth of native plants and fungi in your garden and yard and in wild places. This is good for both you and the wild creatures who share your ecosystem. If you are in the United States, many states have a Native Plant Society chapter you can join.

Don't just pick up any feather or bone you find. In the United States at least, the Migratory Bird Treaty Act prohibits the possession of any feather or other part, as well as nests and eggs, of almost every wild bird in the country. Many countries, states, and other regions have their own laws. You can research wildlife parts laws at http://www.thegreenwolf.com/animal-parts-laws.

Nature also needs those resources! Bones are a very important source of calcium for many animals, including rodents, rabbits, and even deer, as well as plants and fungi. Take only what you need from a carcass, and leave the rest for the wild. Or, if you're an omnivore, consider using bones from meat that you've eaten.

Don't leave crystals or other items around plants after taking some of their leaves. Most of them aren't especially harmful, but it's mostly a feel-good action that doesn't actually help the plant.

Do say thank you by picking up any litter nearby. Extra credit if you learn about the local watershed and how to keep pollution from being flushed out into the waterways and the soil.

Be a Conscientious Consumer

As pagans, it's important for us to be conscientious consumers, especially since so many of our practices involve buying altar tools or spell components. Unfortunately, we often let our esthetic desires take priority over ethical considerations. Here are some ways to do better.

Don't buy crystals unless you know exactly where they came from and who dug them up. The majority of crystals and gemstones on the market were produced by environmentally harmful mining practices, dug up by abused workers who are often enslaved and many of whom are children. While diamonds are the best known example of "blood crystals," the pretty amethysts, fluorites, and other stones in your local New Age shop are also suspect.

Do find ways to collect your own crystals and stones. Talk to your nearest rockhound group or mineralogical society about how to get started. Ask if anyone in your community is getting rid of some crystals, and check thrift stores, too. Secondhand stones are simple enough to cleanse, especially if you consider how much negative energy is stuck to a crystal that was dug up by a seven-year-old slave in a pit mine.

Don't buy cheap statues, candles, Halloween/Samhain decorations, and other items from dollar stores and big-box discount stores. Much like the crystals and minerals we just discussed, these are almost always made by underpaid, abused workers out of eco-unfriendly materials, transported globally on ships that leak pollutants and transport invasive aquatic species in their ballast.

Do buy local and buy secondhand. Buy directly from local artisans…Know that your money is going to someone who is getting a fair wage and may even be self-employed in your community.

Do buy local and buy secondhand. Buy directly from local artisans working in better materials such as beeswax, hand-dyed fabrics, and pottery. Know that your money is going to someone who is getting a fair wage and may even be self-employed in your community. You can even ask for customization!

If you're on a budget, look to your local thrift stores for options. Many of them have candles and candleholders, statues, and other cool trinkets for altars. They also often get bunches of Halloween and other seasonal decorations donated to them year-round. And best of all, you can often find things that aren't in the big-box stores! Again, all they need is a bit of cleansing.

Safe and Respectful Behavior Around Wildlife

We humans are very good at making things all about us. And especially in nature-based religions, we want so badly to feel like we're a part of nature that we inflict our selfish needs onto other beings. Even wanting to attract wildlife so you can see them benefits you more than them, and can be harmful to those creatures.

Don't bother the wildlife. If you encounter animals that don't run when you approach, it probably doesn't mean you have special powers. They likely do the same with other people too, because they think you might have food or they aren't afraid of people. Or they might have rabies. Do you really want to take that chance?

Do maintain a respectful distance from wildlife. Getting too close to wild animals can make them run, which causes them to burn unnecessary calories. Those calories can be the difference between making it through the week or not; a pregnant animal may also miscarry if scared away. Increased human presence makes more sensitive animals such as cougars and elk stay away from feeding grounds and waterways, which is a form of habitat loss for them.

Don't let familiars and other pets roam free. Domestic pets kill millions of wild animals every year, and injure even more. Even if the wild animals hear your pets coming, they still have to deal with the stress of escape. Cats return home with only about a quarter of the animals they actually catch or kill,

> **If you encounter animals that don't run when you approach, it probably doesn't mean you have special powers. They likely do the same with other people too, because they think you might have food or they aren't afraid of people.**

so even if your outdoor cat has never brought a kill home, chances are they've slaughtered numerous songbirds and other wildlife. Moreover, cats and dogs that run free are at serious risk of injury or death due not only to attacks by coyotes and other predators, falls down cliffs, and drowning in waterways but also to getting hit by cars, abused by malicious humans, eating poisons left out for rodents, etc.

Do be responsible with your familiars and pets. Keep cats indoors or in enclosed "catios" in your yard or on your porch. Keep dogs in a fenced yard. (Tying them up is unhealthy for them, both physically and mentally.) Dogs and cats benefit from leash training from an early age and can enjoy frequent walks with you, keeping them safe from outdoor dangers. They'll live longer lives, and your local wildlife will thank you for taking away one of the threats they face.

Don't overly romanticize wildlife. If you're seeing more wildlife than usual, stop making it all about you. Look at the actual reasons they may be coming around more. Did that pair of red-tailed hawks decide to annex your yard as part of their territory this breeding season? Is there a housing development or other construction project going on nearby that's destroying habitat and causing disruptive, scary noise? Are certain species migrating, and your home happens to be along a traditional migration route? Is climate change causing some species to move north to avoid the heat (or south, if you're in the Southern Hemisphere)?

Do learn the natural history of the wildlife around you, as well as that of the plants, fungi, and other living beings they rely on in their ecosystem. Most importantly, learn about the challenges they face in their day-to-day lives, especially those caused by human interference. Then learn about how you can help support them and minimize your own impact while still appreciating the beauty of nature around you.

Stop looking at nature in terms of what you can get out of it, like spell components or magical help. Instead, turn the focus around and consider what you can do to give back to the natural world, which has helped support you every day of your life. Be generous instead of greedy.

．．．．．．．．．．．．

I don't want to sound like a big meanie with all these do's and don'ts, but we really need to be mindful of how and where our spiritual practices can have seriously negative effects on the world around us. By stopping to consider the origin of something you want to do or have, and what the repercussions will be if that happens, you can be a more responsible member of the global community. And that is a much better offering to nature and its beings than a plate of food or a few quartz crystals dropped on the ground.

Lupa (she/her) *is a pagan author, artist, and naturalist in the Pacific Northwest. She has been a practicing pagan since 1996 and is a lifelong nature nerd. She is the author of many books on nature-based paganism and related topics, including* Nature Spirituality From the Ground Up: Connect with Totems in Your Ecosystem (Llewellyn, 2016), The Tarot of Bones (self-published, 2017), *and* Vulture Culture 101: A Book for People Who Like Dead Things (self-published, 2019). *She can be found online at http://www.thegreenwolf.com.*

Illustrator: M. Kathryn Thompson

Adventures in Behavioral Rhetoric: How Do We Deal with Fake News?

Susan Pesznecker

We've all been there—having that moment where a friend, family member, fellow Pagan, or pretty much any human shares an idea or meme or link and we immediately know that something about it isn't right. It might seem so outright insulting or bizarre that it's obviously "off." Or it could be more understated: a date that feels wrong or an odd juxtaposition of images that doesn't really make sense. Whether it's overt or subtle, our radar is alerted.

Or perhaps we're trying to create a blog post or a piece of writing and we realize we're questioning a piece of information we want to use. Or maybe we share something online and discover, too late, that we forgot to check the date and the piece is two years old and no longer relevant.

In this technologically "advanced" era, when it's so easy to find and share information and when we should theoretically be learning from one another, why do so many of us have problems figuring out what's real and reliable and factual and what isn't? Why are people happy to make posts that are derogatory or insulting rather than trying to advance a factual conversation? Why does the public seem more bent on being "right" than being correct? Why is this whole process so fraught?

What's All the Talk about Fake News?

My favorite take on fake news? There's no such thing: it's either news or it isn't, right? But of course that's simplistic, and there are a number of variables at play behind the fake news epidemic. These factors make it hard to find and use good information. They're part of a modern problem making discovery, fact-finding, and respectful human discourse almost impossible.

Facts versus Opinions

A fact is a piece of evidence that can be proven objectively and isn't based on faith, belief, or opinion. Facts can certainly be tied in with faith and belief, but they operate independently of them. Present the same objective, factual information to ten people, and they'll reach the same conclusion about it.

An opinion, in contrast, is a view or judgment formed about an idea. Opinion is subjective and is typically based on belief, opinion, or perspective rather than objective facts or knowledge. The oft-used Pagan expression of "UPG"—Unified Personal Gnosis, i.e., a sudden feeling or revelation experienced by an individual—is a great example of something that can be intensely meaningful but is not at all factual. Present a set of beliefs or opinions to those same ten people, and they'll all weigh the information, taking into account their own varied backgrounds and experiences, and likely reach ten completely different conclusions.

There's absolutely a time and a place for both opinions and facts, and they come together when we share experiences and ideas and think through creative options. But when we're talking about truth and reliability, we want facts. We want that anchor point where everyone can come together. Shared knowledge. Common ground.

But some people, presented with facts, still deny them and cling to what they want to believe rather than what's right in front of them. Why are humans often resistant to change, and why do many people seem to shy away from finding reliable facts?

It's All about the Evolution

For the most part, and particularly during our early life, we form opinions through our contact with trusted family, friends, and mentors. We model what we see and hear from them. Children and young people form a sense of who they are through these contacts, taking clues from those around them. Eventually, that growing sense of self, along with growth-related behavior and changes in the brain, leads people to make their own decisions about what they believe, what's important to them, and how they want to live their lives. These decisions evolve and change from those opinions held as children.

But while this kind of evolution is typical of childhood, humans— and especially adults—really don't like change, whether it means changing opinions, beliefs, faith, or even allegiance to a specific fact set. Changing one's mind means accepting a new set of facts and being able to directly apply those facts to one's life. This isn't easy, and complicating it further are a number of factors that make changing one's mind even tougher.

Trust is a big one. We're most likely to accept facts from people we rely on and trust. Humans learn best by experience, but our initial exposure to facts typically comes from people around us. We take that further, testing the facts, trying them out in different settings, and then firming up our own decisions about them. The process begins with trust.

Homophily is closely tied to trust. Homophily refers to surrounding ourselves with people who think and reason in much the same way that we do—a collective posse in which we find commonality. There's safety in numbers, and keeping company with like-minded people makes us comfortable.

And, of course, our own knowledge plays an important factor. As we gain more life experience, we test our belief system against factual knowledge gained over years. When we're lucky, it works. The young student studying Wicca learns a set of specific practices and traditions, and as they grow in spirit, they find that their beliefs align with the realities of daily practice—ideally. But what if the idealistic young Wiccan-to-be joins a coven, full of starry-eyed enthusiasm, and is asked to do or think or believe in something that completely stands in opposition to the way they've always lived their life. What then?

A Mind Is a Terrible Thing to Change

Just as trust helps us form our opinions and accept truth, low trust helps those processes unravel and makes us look in other directions. We see this in politics when a group of people lose trust in a powerful figure and then are willing to accept a lie, manipulated truth, or conspiracy theory about the person—especially if the information makes that person look bad. Once trust is lost, it's very hard to get it back.

Existing beliefs and opinions can make it hard for us to entertain a new set of facts. If a fact presented to us conflicts with one of our deeply held beliefs, we're unlikely to change our mind. Reinforcing this with confirmation bias or with the support of a charismatic leader, mentor, or public figure makes it even more true. We've seen this in the Pagan community when the occasional elder has been found to have broken the law or violated ethical behavior, even when the facts are clear, there are those who adore the elder and simply can't accept it. "I know they'd never do that," they say.

And speaking of charisma, the world is full of situations where that person becomes the shiny object people want to follow but then turns out to be not so nice, typically abusing their power or the people worshipping at their feet. I knew a woman who called herself priestess of her coven. She would lure people into her circle with promises of community but then require them to more or less become her personal servants—forcing them to show their allegiance by cleaning her house and doing her laundry, and withholding their advancement if they failed to cooperate. People in these situations often stay with the charismatic abuser for long periods of time, even defending them to others.

Cognitive dissonance is the ability to have contrasting thoughts about an idea and to hold these closely in one's mind without resolving them. An example might be staying with a Heathen kindred you're comfortable with while simultaneously becoming aware that two of the members have ties to racist or white supremacist organizations.

You rationalize your comfort because you like the group, but you worry about racism being integrated into the clan. "I'm not racist. Those aren't *my* positions," you might say to yourself. This is cognitive dissonance in action. You're unlikely to change your mind as long as the scales tip in your favor.

Confirmation bias occurs when the people we surround ourselves with (homophily) agree with us and support us, giving us little motivation to think differently. Confirmation bias provides the comfort of being part of a group but also allows those social dynamics to override facts as well as the best outcome. We see this in people who cleave hard to partisan politics or who vote in line with a certain person or position rather than considering each idea and making individual best decisions.

Repetition often goes along with negative charismatic behavior. Simply put, if you say that something is true loudly enough and often enough, people will start to accept it as truth, even when it isn't. They won't question the repetition and will come to accept it as factual.

Here's one of my favorite examples of cognitive bias: the Dunning-Kruger effect. This effect says that people who often know the least about something tend to be extremely confident that they know everything they need to manage a situation. This psychological phenomenon is present in all of us to some extent, especially in children. It becomes a problem when it persists into adulthood or is used to avoid reality. As a nurse, I once reviewed a book of herbal medicine and found a number of problems in terms of how the herbs were being used and applied. But when I shared my medicine and physiology-based comments, the writer became upset and focused on her past years as an herbal "expert," saying she knew everything about her practices and any different advice was irrelevant and insulting.

Motivated reasoning ties in with Dunning-Kruger, too. This suggests that people interpret new information and facts in a way that confirms their existing worldviews, beliefs, identities, and needs—even if that contradicts how they think. A recent example was the discovery that most crystals used by New Age practitioners have been mined or obtained unethically and often in sweatshop-esque conditions. Yet people who love to use and buy crystals rationalize that they only get their stones from "reliable" sources, even when studies show that most vendor stocks come from the same locations.

What Role Does Technology Play in Decision Making?

If people struggle with understanding the differences between fact and opinion and truth and lies, the current technological era only makes it worse. The explosion of technology and "freedom" of information gives us unprecedented access to information and to sharing it with others. Even so, we often get it wrong. Technology augments all of the problems involved with finding, assessing, and sharing information, as well as with the intricacies of forming and changing opinions.

Probably the biggest problem with technology is how easy it is to find information. That may sound like a contradiction, but if you google a search term and get three million hits in three seconds, are you going to read each one of those to find out which one is best? Impossible. Chances are, you'll pick one of the first hits on the list, particularly if it agrees with what you already know. The filter-bubble problem makes this harder because it gives you a list of results that it thinks you "want" to see. Anytime we search, click a link, or order something online, the browser stores information about what we did and uses algorithms to make conclusions about us. These conclusions are then used to respond to all of our online activities. The pros? It becomes easier to find information online. The cons? The scope of what we find is narrower and more limited, as it's tightly focused. This is a poor way to find a broad swath of answers in response to a question.

The volume of information we can find and the speed with which we find it is a problem too. Taking information from top hits is easy, and that's what most people do. On top of that, they often don't check the date or assess the material. Very few people actually read their materials through. And then…they share them. Our urge to share and disseminate information rapidly makes it even more likely the information will be wrong. If the material hasn't been read and vetted and is quickly shared, misinformation may be spread. Plus, many people edit or modify information to share only what they agree with, amplifying bias within the material.

Our urge to share and disseminate information rapidly makes it even more likely the information will be wrong. If the material hasn't been read and vetted and is quickly shared, misinformation may be spread.

Tension between digital natives and digital immigrants plays a role as well. Digital natives are those born in the era of technology, while digital immigrants arrived on its supposed shores and had to assimilate into the world of technology. Recent research from the Stanford Graduate School of Education "finds that young and otherwise digital-savvy students can easily be duped. They have a difficult time distinguishing news articles from advertisements as well as identifying the source and reliability of information they encounter" (Spikes 2017). But the digital natives aren't alone in this. A newer study suggests that while young people may have trouble sorting out and sharing fake news, it's also a problem for digital immigrants (Stewart 2019). It's easy to see that many people are having trouble navigating the perils of digital factfinding.

How Can We Do Better?

It may sound like we've dug ourselves a deep hole with no way out. But there's lots we can do to become better finders, users, and sharers of information, as well as more ways to shape and modify our own opinions and positions.

Begin by resolving that with any new piece of information, you'll do the following:

1. Check the date on the information and decide if it's appropriate.

2. Read the entire article. Before using material, you'd better be confident of its quality.

3. Fact-check the article *before* sharing it. Don't risk propagating misinformation.

> **Check the date on the information and decide if it's appropriate.... Fact-check the article *before* sharing it. Don't risk propagating misinformation.**

Assess Material Using the CRAP Test

A simple way to assess materials is to use the **CRAP test**, an acronym for a test used nationwide by librarians. Work through these steps:

Currency: When and where was the material published? Is it relevant? Has it been revised or updated? Does your topic require newer information or is this adequate?

Reliability: Does the information work for your purpose? Does it answer your questions? Does it reach out to the correct audience? Is it written at an appropriate level of complexity? Have you looked at other sources to determine that this one is best?

Authority: Who is the author? What are their credentials? Are they the right person(s) to publish this material? Do they have other publications? Do they provide contact information allowing you to reach them?

Purpose/Point of View: What's the point of the piece? Is it trying to teach, tell, entertain, or something else? Is this congruent with your own intentions? Is the information aimed more toward presenting facts, giving opinion, or disseminating propaganda? Are facts presented in support of the information? Is the tone factual and professional rather than insulting or negative?

Fact-Checking Sites

The web is also full of fact-checkers—sites that allow you to ask your own questions or type in specific information. Here are a few:

- Associated Press (AP) Fact Checker, www.apnews.com/AP FactCheck

- Fact-Checking at the Poynter, https://www.poynter.org/media -news/fact-checking/

- FactCheck.org

- Harvard's "Research Guide to Fake News, Misinformation, and Propaganda," https://guides.library.harvard.edu/fake

- National Public Radio (NPR) Fact Check, https://www.npr.org /sections/politics-fact-check

- PolitiFact, https://www.politifact.com/

- Snopes, https://www.snopes.com/

- Washington Post Fact Checker, https://www.washingtonpost .com/news/fact-checker/

Bypass the Filter Bubble

When using the internet, here are some ways to bypass the filter bubble:

- Use ad blockers.

- Use VPNs and incognito browsers.

- Delete search histories after each online session.

- Do work without logging in as much as possible.

- Delete or block cookies.

- Read objective, reliable news sites that offer a wide range of perspectives and positions.

How Do We Motivate People to Question Their Beliefs and Thought Processes?

It's downright hard to get people to change their way of thinking. But if you're armed with facts and truth and want to get through to them, here are a few guidelines:

1. They must trust you. If they don't, they'll have absolutely no reason to believe you or accept the facts. Along this same line, the right person must introduce the right information at the right time. If you're not the right person, find someone who is.

2. Provide facts—in a nonthreatening way.

3. Using visual examples such as photographs, charts, or other images may be more effective than using written materials or "lecturing."

4. Change usually doesn't happen quickly. The information must be repeated.

Practicing Good information Literacy

Information literacy refers to the ability to correctly assess the factual nature of sources; the ability to assess the authority, credibility, and reliability of sources; and the ability to use source materials ethically and correctly to support a position.

As a writer or someone who may be in a position of teaching or leading others, you can model good information literacy in a number of ways:

1. Write objectively, fairly, and with a mind open to other possibilities.

2. Show that you can accept the positions and disagreements of others.

3. Avoid using language that is biased or unkind or blames others.

4. Support your ideas with reliable facts.

5. Avoid supporting ideas with opinion, faith, or belief alone.

6. Make sure your work is as error-free as possible—errors undermine a reader's confidence.

7. Handle sources correctly, citing them in your work and gathering them in a list at the end. Failing to do so is a kind of plagiarism.

In today's world, we're also faced with the demands of the digital age and its influence on knowledge and decision making. Many of these aspects are beyond our control, but if we do our best to handle information honestly and correctly, only good can result.

Notes

Spikes, Michael. "Making Sense of the News: Distinguishing News from Sponsored Content." BillMoyers.com, February 22, 2017. https://billmoyers.com/story/making-sense-news-distinguishing-news -sponsored-content/.

Stewart, Emily. "People over 65 Are the Most Likely to Share Fake News on Facebook, Study Finds." Vox, January 10, 2019. https://www.vox .com/policy-and-politics/2019/1/10/18175913/facebook-fake-news -2016-election-republicans-trump.

Susan Pesznecker is a mother, writer, nurse, and college English professor living in the beautiful Pacific Northwest with her poodles. An initiated Druid, green magick devoteé, and amateur herbalist, Sue loves reading, writing, cooking, travel, and anything having to do with the outdoors. Previous works include Crafting Magick with Pen and Ink, The Magickal Retreat, *and* Yule: Recipes & Lore for the Winter Solstice. *She's a regular contributor to the Llewellyn annuals. Follow her on Instagram as Susan Pesznecker.*

Illustrator: Bri Hermanson

Pop-Culture Witches Have Something to Teach Us

Deborah Lipp

I'm sitting at my desk (I work from home) and the Wicked Queen from *Snow White and the Seven Dwarfs* is looking down on me, holding out a tempting apple. Next to her, Scarlet Witch, of *Avengers* fame, smiles.

My home is full of witches—some highly collectible, some quite personal, some pure kitsch. They include several Disney witches (such as Maleficent from *Sleeping Beauty* and the Wicked Queen as queen and also as old hag), numerous

iterations of both Glinda and the Wicked Witch of the West from *The Wizard of Oz*, a couple of Lego witches, and both of my goddaughters (unrelated to each other) in witch costumes. A little statuette of three witches reminds me of three Wiccan sisters I know, so I painted their hair color to match my friends'.

Is there any purpose to these witches other than décor? Although I don't use them formally in any sort of ritual, I think the answer is yes.

Pop culture gets under our skin. It speaks to us. From our earliest days, we are exposed to everything from Grimm fairy tales to nursery rhymes to Disney. Whatever we may consciously know about witchcraft, these images were there first. Pop-culture witches serve a complex function in our psyches. As much as we say, truthfully, that as Wiccans we are not in the business of poisoning anyone with apples or cursing them with spindles, and I've never stolen anyone's shoes, ruby or otherwise, I'd suggest that if we hadn't found some resonance with these fictional depictions of witchcraft, we might never have found and connected with the real thing. What I mean is, many of us were first drawn in by the word *witch*, and only later found Neopagan witchcraft.

For me, the first connection is a feminist one. Women of the era I grew up in had little agency in popular fiction. Snow White barely speaks a word in her own movie. She cooks and cleans, is exiled, and requires a prince to rescue her. Until very recently, Disney princesses were remarkably passive. So is Dorothy in *The Wizard of Oz*—she talks a good game, but in the long run, she gets conked on the head and then runs around being told what to do and asking for help.

Where, then, were strong, independent role models for me? One answer is *witches*. The Wicked Queen from *Snow White* had her own castle, a beautiful gown and jewels, a magic mirror, a huntsman to order around, and a laboratory full of spell books and potions. She was cool. Okay, evil. But cool. As she looks down at me from her perch on my desk, I feel empowered. She is handing me not an apple, but strength and self-sufficiency.

Another connection to the fictional witch is that of the outsider. Historically, a witch (or folk magic practitioner) was quite literally on the outside, often living on the outskirts of her community. The imagery clustered around this outsider is that of an oddball, someone needed but not entirely trusted. Lots of us can connect to that. For that energy I have Maleficent, strong and proud and absolutely refusing to be ostracized. In *Sleeping Beauty*, three fairy godmothers are invited to celebrate Aurora's christening, but Maleficent is snubbed. When you or I are insulted in this way, we stay home from the party and sulk. Not Maleficent. She arrives in style (not to mention, in a ball of green flame). She is regal and commanding, says her piece, and storms out in a rage. Her truth is, I *will not be abandoned. I will not be ignored. It is not okay to mistreat me because I am different or because you are scared.* As such, I think she has a lot of healing to offer.

While the Wicked Queen and Maleficent offer universal messages that many of us can relate to, my relationship with Scarlet Witch is far more personal. As a comic book fan from the time I could read, I found in this character someone like me in very particular ways.

> **Historically, a witch (or folk magic practitioner) was quite literally on the outside, often living on the outskirts of her community. The imagery clustered around this outsider is that of an oddball, someone needed but not entirely trusted. Lots of us can connect to that. For that energy I have Maleficent, strong and proud and absolutely refusing to be ostracized.**

Most people know Scarlet Witch (a.k.a. Wanda Maximoff) from the *Avengers* movies. In the comics, she was first an X-Men villain before becoming an Avenger. Her mutant power resembled, but wasn't identical to, witchcraft—until, in the 1970s, she decided to study with another awesome fictional witch, Agatha Harkness.

Wanda was Romani, Eastern European, and had a pile of dark, curly hair. I was a Jewish girl growing up in a suburb with almost no other Jews. In the comics, the female heroes were almost all blonde or ginger, often patrician, with white-bread names like Jean Grey, Sue Storm, and Janet van Dyne. Wanda stood out in that crowd just as I stood out in the 'burbs, and I adored her. (I was terribly disappointed by the fair-haired, green-eyed casting of Elizabeth Olsen as the movies' Scarlet Witch.) Wanda was me as a superhero, and when she studied witchcraft, even better.

As I walk around my home, seeing witches on a shelf here, in a framed picture there, I am in touch with my childhood delight at these characters, with my love of their strength, power, and individuality. Often I stop and look at one or another and feel awakened to the threads within my psyche that led me to Wicca so many years ago. All of these witches have a connection to me that is serious but also playful. The fun is part of the point. Most of my friends are Wiccan—we're a fun-loving, raucous bunch as a rule. But Wiccans can occasionally be far too serious, and embracing something this obviously silly is a good counterweight for that.

I've described three of my witches and what they mean to me. One is a reframing of womanhood, a vision that half the population could potentially enjoy. One is asserting the power of the outsider, something many, many people can find healing in. And one is deeply personal, specific to my own childhood.

Meditation on Fictional Witches

What might fictional witches mean to you? Here's a meditation to help you find out.

Prepare yourself for meditation as you normally do. Get in a comfortable position in a quiet space, with no risk of interruption. Light incense or candles if this is your habit. Ground and center yourself.

Now reach into your childhood. Allow your mind to wander gently back in time. If you've changed your name as an adult, try saying your childhood name or nickname to help bring memories to the fore.

Once you've reached a place where you're in touch with your younger self, remember the first witches you encountered. Were they in fairy tales? Movies? Art? What do you remember about them? Let the images wash over you.

Now focus in on one witch, a favorite. Turn her over in your mind. Make her vivid. Recall everything you can about her. As you do so, look within. How does it make you feel to spend time with her? What are your emotions? What are your thoughts?

Now allow yourself to imagine you are this witch. Is that a satisfying thought? How do you feel? Powerful, beautiful, sexy, scary? What are the words that come most easily to mind?

Before ending your meditation, be sure to bring yourself forward into adulthood. Call yourself by your present, adult name. Re-center yourself and remember you are grounded. Then open your eyes.

You can end this meditation by journaling about it. You might wish to repeat this exercise a few times to find multiple images that really resonate with you, perhaps meditating on a different witch each time. Or one time might provide all the information you seek.

Now that you've found the magic of one or more witches, you can choose to populate your life with them if you feel they have qualities that are meaningful for you—or just for fun.

Other Pop-Culture Figures

Witches aren't the only magical characters from pop culture, of course. My ex adored wizards like Gandalf and Merlin. They spoke deeply to him. I suspect they offered an empowering counterbalance to the kind of man he was "supposed" to grow up to be but never could, a way of being a strong man without being macho or athletic.

Pop-culture figures can be any gender or age. They can be from any sort of art, real or fantastical. Certainly there are many Pagans who connect deeply with fairies, elves, hobbits, and vampires. Feel free to repeat the previous meditation with any fictional creature who speaks to you.

I have a deep connection with fairies, and there are almost as many fairies in my home as witches. In fact, I have several fairy tattoos (but no witches…yet). Fairies, to me, represent a kind of untouchable freedom. This is, again, a very personal image, and quite unlike the idea of fairies that many other fairy lovers have. And that's okay. The important part here is to look inside, find the meaning, bring it forth, and celebrate it.

Deborah Lipp's *most recent books are* Magical Power for Beginners *and* Tarot Interactions. *Her earlier works include* The Study of Witchcraft, The Elements of Ritual, The Way of Four, The Way of Four Spellbook, Merry Meet Again, *and* The Ultimate James Bond Fan Book. *One of these things is not like the other.*

Deborah has been teaching Wicca, magic, and the occult for over thirty years. She became a Witch and a High Priestess in the 1980s, as an initiate of the Gardnerian tradition of Wicca. She's been published in many Pagan publications, including newWitch, PanGaia, *and* Green Egg.

In "real life," Deborah is a senior business analyst. She lives with her spouse, Melissa, and an assortment of cats in Jersey City, NJ, three blocks from a really great view of Freedom Tower. Deborah reads and teaches Tarot, solves and designs puzzles, watches old movies, hand-paints furniture, and dabbles in numerous handcrafts.

Follow Deborah on Twitter: @DebLippAuthor.

Illustrator: Tim Foley

To Hex or Not to Hex

Michelle Skye

Be honest. You've thought about it: hexing the company that pollutes your local waterway, the gossip at work who spreads lies about you and costs you a promotion, or the soccer coach who is revealed to be an abuser. As magic practitioners, we've all been there. We know we have the power to effect change, but maybe we're a little nervous to exercise that power. A lot of the time, we separate ourselves from the bigger picture, rationalizing that "it's none of my business." In today's world of social media, the #MeToo movement, the Black Lives Matter movement, and worldwide political hypocrisy, many witches and magic practitioners are taking a stand. In recent years, news articles heralded the hexing of Donald Trump, Brett Kavanaugh, and other members of the radical right by "resistance witches" and other groups that gather at well-known metaphysical shops. Hearing of these hexes, other magic practitioners took to their blogs and public formats of discussion to decry the actions of these witches, stating that hexing is immoral and harmful to the pagan community at large. Hexing is a topic of contention that has many ties to the witchcraft community, so let's take a look at what hexing actually is.

What Is Hexing?

In its simplest definition, hexing is the use of magical power to harm or hurt another person, organization, or company. It does not have to be defensive or done in response to an action against you or someone (or something) you love, although usually it is. In its purest form, a hex could be placed on someone just because you don't like them. Simple as that.

Hexing, or cursing, is one of the oldest forms of magic. There are examples of hexes or curses carved into 130 lead sheets at the ruins of Bath, England. Petitioners would pay to have a scribe write a particular curse on a small sheet of lead. Then they would throw the lead sheet into the baths, dedicated to the goddess Sulis Minerva. These curses were varied but included the inability to have children or to sleep. Another tablet requested that the perpetrator lose his eyes and his mind. One person who stole a slave was cursed with turning into water!

Since a majority of these curses focus on items that had been stolen and do not traditionally name a specific person, it has been suggested that those who created the curses at the baths of Sulis Minerva may have been from a lower economic station. In other words, they did not have guards to protect their items and could not count on the government to help them recover their stolen goods. Therefore, they felt that their only option for justice was in cursing or hexing the individual.

I think this imbalance of power is at the heart of hexing. Powerful people don't typically go around hexing people. They use their money and connections to influence the society around them. In short, they have no need for hexing because they have the means to effect change in other ways. They buy judges or keep litigation in the courts for years, decimating the savings of the other party. They chat with their college roommates or family friends in order to achieve their preferred goals. They are able to create the life of their wishes through socially acceptable means. No hexing necessary.

The connection of hexing to the disenfranchised explains why hexing is also connected to witches and witchcraft. Witches are a segment of society that were (and, some would argue, still are) only marginally accepted. In the Middle Ages, curses were said to take the form of blighted crops, lame horses, and dry cows. Lone women (or witches) were often accused of casting these curses and were punished because of this belief. These so-called witches were often widows, knowledgeable in herbs and with little to no family support. With no masculine figure to shield them and support their actions, they did not fill a traditionally accepted role in the village. This made them vulnerable to attack. Erica Jong, in her books *What Do Women Want?* and *Witches*, writes that "the more disempowered people are, the more they long for magic, which explains why magic becomes the province of women in a sexist society."

Keeping all of this in mind, including the fact that curses were used in the cradle of civilization in Mesopotamia as well as in ancient Egypt, Rome, and Greece, and were placed in bibles by the early Christian Church, why are people shocked by the idea of utilizing a hex in modern times? Why the criminalization of the magical form of cursing? In order to understand the dislike of and reticence toward hexing on the part of some magic practitioners, you need to understand two basic concepts: harm none and free will.

Harm None

"An it harm none, do what ye will" is the short version of the Wiccan Rede, first stated publicly in a 1964 speech by well-known Wiccan writer and advocate Doreen Valiente. In a nutshell, the Wiccan Rede gives practitioners (specifically those following the religion of Wicca) the right to act in any way they wish, as long as their actions do no harm. The practitioner should act in accordance with their highest ideals and their truest desires, not just in relation to a specific time and place but in connection with their highest self.

Any action, be it magical or mundane, is to be judged according to the possible harm it could cause. Some practitioners read this to mean harm only against themselves, while others view harm in relation to themselves and all living things, and still others see harm in relation to all possible things and experiences. This ambiguity in the Wiccan Rede leaves it open to interpretation by the individual. In the case of performing hex magic, many Wiccans stay clear of it since hexing is meant to specifically hurt or cause harm to another and thus would go against the Wiccan Rede.

Free Will

Free will is the ability of every sentient being to choose their own pathway in life, a concept that is central to modern Western culture. It exults in having choice, outside of external coercion. This includes the belief that each individual does not have a predisposed life that has been determined ahead of their birth by an omnipotent deity. Many philosophers and psychologists wonder if we do, in actuality, have free will, as we are all subconsciously influenced by societal norms and familial expectations placed on us.

Free will plays an important role in magic as the practitioner exercises their free will to create a desired outcome. With free will, your magic is powerful as you exercise your right to influence and shape your path.

However, free will is equally important magically when other individuals become a central focus of your magic. In the case of hexing magic or love magic aimed at a specific person, the magic practitioner interferes in the other person's free will by imposing their magical will upon the other. The magic supersedes the free will of the individual, and they behave in ways that are outside of their desires.

Now, it is important to note that these two concepts—harm none and free will—are not universal. They are specific to modern witchcraft and Wicca. These ideas were not wholly accepted (nor even thought of) by medieval or ancient magic practitioners, and some modern practitioners view them with derision. They believe that these general guidelines are only for those who follow a specific pagan religion (Wicca), not for all practitioners of magic. Ultimately, the decision to hex or not to hex is up to the individual.

Binding

In my opinion, hexing, or cursing, is an acceptable form of magic—for some people. Not everyone is going to feel comfortable performing negative magic or accepting the consequences that may or may not come from such magical action. It's important to look at yourself and see what kinds of wounds or scars you carry, what sorts of things trigger your neuroses or inner critic, what outside behaviors cause reactive actions, and where you stand in your personal growth. In short, you have to know yourself in order to make the decision to hex or not to hex.

My own views on hexing and cursing have fluctuated over time, but they almost always come back to the same idea. I don't choose to curse or hex, but sometimes I do bind. Binding is a form of magic that stops the other person from performing negative actions toward you or toward a family member or friend. I choose not to curse or hex mostly because of the 1996 movie *The Craft*. For real. I don't want to end up like Nancy at the end of that movie, completely crazy because

I couldn't control the energy that I invoked. I know my limitations, and unleashing the kind of anger that is inherent in a curse or hex is not something I can handle. I know that I already have anger issues from past lives (and past experiences) of persecution and powerlessness. I spend a great deal of my time working to transmute that anger into peace, calm, and joy. Anger is a knee-jerk response for me that doesn't solve anything and usually causes problems in the long run, although it has taught me a good deal, including how to breathe through the red-hot anger into the cool blue of orderly action—on occasion. I'm still working on this lesson!

Bindings, however, aren't necessarily about anger. They're more about removing someone's energy from your life. They protect. They separate. They create distance.... I see bindings as a cosmic timeout, a chance for you to get the negative energy out of your space.

Bindings, however, aren't necessarily about anger. They're more about removing someone's energy from your life. They protect. They separate. They create distance. I understand that you are technically messing with someone's free will. However, sometimes, after you've tried everything you can think of, there doesn't appear to be any other solution. I see bindings as a cosmic timeout, a chance for you to get the negative energy out of your space. So, like a timeout, a binding shouldn't last forever, just long enough for both parties to cool down.

A lot of people bind by using a string and a picture of the person, like the Earth-aligned witch in The Craft. I have written people's names down on paper and placed them in a plastic bag in the freezer in order to get their energy out of my life. Currently, my favorite binding technique is to create an avatar (or *Mii*) of the person on the Wii gaming system. I then take the Mii out of the game and place it in the Mii Parade, which I affectionately refer to as the Wii Timeout Healing Room. It's not an uncomfortable place but is just rather gray, although the Miis do walk or run continually while they're in the room. I guess that's what keeps them focused on something other than me!

Protection Magic

Another form of magic that is closely connected to hexing, cursing, and binding is protection magic. Protection magic is done on another person in order to protect them from negativity. You might do protection magic on yourself if someone is gossiping about you or spreading lies about you. Protection magic can also be utilized to protect another person who is being cursed or spoken of in a negative fashion.

When I was a young, fledgling Wiccan, I had a non-Wiccan friend who practiced subconscious magic. I can hear all the groans now…Subconscious magic? Is that even a thing? After all, magic requires focus, intent, and belief. *Subconscious* indicates someone who is not consciously aware and has no intent. Or does it? I am using subconscious magic as another word for wish magic. You know, that kid-like belief in wishing on a star or blowing out birthday candles. There is an intent and a minimal belief that it will work, but nobody calls it magic or really works to make the desire happen.

My friend did this sort of magic a lot, usually in relation to former boyfriends. She would lie in bed before falling asleep and wish ill will upon the boy who dumped her. She would hope and pray that the former boyfriends would feel all the hurt and pain that she felt. And they did. One boy had his car blow up with all of his worldly possessions inside. Another got in a serious car accident that caused him to be physically harmed. My friend was cursing these boys, even though she would not have called it by that name.

At one point this friend started dating a friend of mine from work. They were ecstatically happy—until they weren't, and he broke up with her. She was devastated and started her old ritual of lying in bed at night and wishing ill upon her former boyfriend—*my* friend. I was frantic.

I didn't know what to do. He was set to go work on a historic replica ship that was going to cruise down the East Coast and through the Caribbean for the winter. When my female friend started mentioning hurricanes and drownings in casual conversation with me, I could see the hexing pattern continuing and I didn't know what to do.

I made the decision to protect my male friend rather than bind my female friend. I thought it would make sense to protect the ship from her ill wishes, since she was talking about devastation on a ship-wide level rather than just in relation to him. So I crafted a magical talisman in the ethers that would protect the ship from harm—and it worked! Though in a way that I could not have predicted. The ship never left the dock, and my male friend missed out on a once-in-a-lifetime opportunity. It never occurred to me to bind my female friend. I was too hung up on the rules of Wicca, which, at the time, seemed like the best choice for me. If confronted with the same scenario now, would

> **At one point this friend started dating a friend of mine from work. They were ecstatically happy—until they weren't, and he broke up with her. She was devastated and started her old ritual of lying in bed at night and wishing ill upon her former boyfriend—*my* friend. . . . I made the decision to protect my male friend rather than bind my female friend.**

I handle it differently? Probably. There would be a lot more discussion with my female friend, helping her find more positive ways to heal. But if that didn't work, I know I'd take some magical action.

. . . .

Magic is intrinsically tied to the individual practitioner and to the specific situation in which we find ourselves. The choice to hex, curse, bind, or protect will depend on the individual and the circumstances surrounding them at that particular moment in time. The spellcaster's emotional, physical, and mental state have to be considered before any magic is chosen. Taking time to assess these parts of the self is key to deciding which type of magic to cast (or to forgo magical action entirely!).

Every magical act has consequences. If you are true to yourself and your beliefs in that given moment, you will be willing and able to accept whatever consequences manifest in your life. There really is no right or wrong answer to the magical question of whether to hex or not. It's your choice. Take some time to mull it over, assess your inner landscape, talk with friends, read articles and blogs, and then do (or don't do) what feels right for you.

Michelle Skye *is a dedicated tree-hugging, magic-wielding, goddess-loving Pagan. While she is best known for her three goddess books, God-dess Alive, Goddess Afoot, and Goddess Aloud, she also works closely with many gods and male magic practitioners. Michelle is fond of reading (a lot!), rainbows, crows, oracle decks, walks in the woods, Middle Eastern dance, spellwork, grunge music, silver jewelry (especially if it's sparkly), and quirky '80s movies. She creates crafts and spells with her magic circle, the Crafty Witches, and celebrates the sabbats with her family coven at home. She has been spinning magic into the world her whole life but has been following the Pagan path for just over twenty years.*

Illustrator: Bri Hermanson

Rediscovering the Maiden as a Crone

Kerri Connor

My Maiden years were not spiritual. Young, vibrant, sexual, rebellious—yes. But not spiritual. Spirituality was not a part of my life. I didn't even know it was missing.

I knew that the religious beliefs my parents wanted to cement in me had never felt right. They didn't fit. The Evangelical Protestantism they wanted me so desperately to believe in left me with too many questions and far too few answers. Their religion taught me nothing about spirituality. It was a concept I was not familiar with.

I knew my beliefs were different the first time I saw my mother's spirit on the night of her funeral, as she stood at the foot of my bed. I had been pleading to be able to see her again, and when the pink shimmer appeared at the end of my bed, I first threw the blanket over my head. When I peeked, she was still there, and I ended up crying and running from my room. I didn't dare tell my father what I had seen. I knew that if the things the Bible said were true, then seeing my mom's spirit was a bad thing. My pastor confirmed this was bad because that's how he responded to eight-year-old me when I told him about my mom's visit. Her visit had scared me, but my pastor's words scarred me.

I made sure not to see or hear my mother's spirit (or anyone else's) again for many years.

In my mid-teens, when my rebellion against my father and stepmother had reached the "I don't care what they think at all" level, I, like many other teenage girls of the era, began to dabble with a Ouija board.

The first time I placed my hands on a planchette, I knew there was something different going on.

I felt different.

I learned I could communicate with the spirits quite easily, and I could answer questions when I wasn't on the board even faster than the people controlling the board could. It was as if I could predict the answers. Only these weren't simple predictions—they were words, thoughts, information that would just appear in my mind.

I could communicate with my mother and other spirits, but I didn't know how to control it. I had shut off the ability for many years, and when I turned it back on, it poured through the floodgates.

Eventually, in my quest for information, I learned more about spirit boards, then about Spiritualism, and finally about Wicca. This was the '80s, so there wasn't a ton of information out there. Neither was there an internet. Finding information was hard, and information about Pagan pathways other than Wicca was pretty much nonexistent in my little rural corner of the state of Illinois.

When the mid-1990s hit and information was becoming more readily available, I had three young children and two divorces, and I felt very much the Mother and no longer the Maiden. By the time I learned about the three aspects of the Goddess, I felt I had already missed out on the connection with the Maiden. That part of my life was over, and I didn't feel commonalities with her in her different incarnations.

I worked with Mother figures—Gaia, Danu, Demeter, Isis. These were figures I could relate to. They knew my struggles. I found comfort and knowledge from them.

After hitting menopause early and becoming a grandmother at the age of forty-two, and just two years later being diagnosed with breast cancer, I quickly found myself moving on from the Mother to the Crone. I felt old, but I had also learned so much about life that the Crone felt fitting despite my biological age. Cerridwen and the Morrigan became my go-to goddesses. I spent over six years working with them when one night out in my hot tub, I had an experience very different from any I'd ever had before.

Enter the Maiden

For those not familiar with some of my more recent writings, I am a firm believer in the use of cannabis for medical, recreational, and spiritual use. For those who are familiar with my writing, it should come as no surprise that my late-night hot tub time is often used for cannabis-assisted meditations and peak experiences. (A peak experience occurs when you hit true "oneness" with the universe.)

It was during one of those sessions that I felt the overwhelming presence of a deity I hadn't experienced before. A strong floral scent, followed by an introduction, led me to my first encounter with Blodeuwedd.

While I was familiar with Blodeuwedd's story, I had never worked with her. I found her sudden appearance in my life rather surprising. Obviously, though, she had something to teach me, so I began working with her.

Blodeuwedd is the Welsh goddess who was created from flowers by the magicians Math and Gwydion. She was made to be the wife of their nephew Llew Llaw Gyffes, because he was unable to marry any mortal woman due to a curse by his mother, Arianrhod. Eventually Blodeuwedd fell in love with another man, Gronw Pebyr, and the two plotted Llew's demise. Long story short, Llew was saved and Blodeuwedd was turned into an owl as punishment for her "betrayal."

Blodeuwedd was created for someone else. She was never given a choice of who to be or whom to be with. She wasn't her own person. She had no free will. When her eyes were opened to her situation, she began to grow and change. She wanted more. She rebelled and stood up for herself. When she tried to eliminate the man she came to view as her captor, she was punished.

While I was able to feel a connection to Blodeuwedd through memories of my younger self, it still took a while to catch what she was trying to convey to me in my present life. I finally put two and two together and realized she was telling me there were parts of

my younger self, my Maiden self, that I had failed to incorporate into my present, and I needed to do this in order to be more successful in my future. I had the Mother and Crone aspects down and well incorporated, but there were aspects of my earliest self that needed to be integrated.

This revelation led to the next one: what aspects I was missing.

Finding those missing aspects took remembering and reflection, some of it joyful, some extremely painful. Who had I been thirty-plus years ago? Who was I before I was someone else's mother? Who was I to me?

What I soon realized was that I had grown complacent—extremely complacent. For decades I had lived my life for others and not for myself. For years I had let others dictate what was appropriate, proper, necessary. I had allowed others to walk all over me—whether they realized it or not. I had allowed others to take advantage of me—whether they realized it or not.

I began taking back bits and pieces of myself that I had given away. The same old same old was no longer acceptable. I had reached the end of my rope and began insisting that I be treated as a deserving human being and not an emotional punching bag.

I began putting my wants, needs, and priorities first. Most of all, I put an end to any and all gaslighting attempts against me.

I finally realized that for decades I had allowed myself to be a victim of gaslighting by family and so-called friends. I had allowed myself to be manipulated instead of standing up for myself, as I didn't want to hurt anyone else's feelings. I had tolerated this treatment for far too long from far too many directions. I had been treated like a doormat, and often by those who should have treated me far better.

Until I just stopped. Until I said, "I've had it. I'm done."

Blodeuwedd had come to me to remind me, to show me, who I had once been. The younger me, the Maiden me, would never have allowed the type of treatment I had condoned for so many years. She came to wake up my Maiden self, to help me reclaim the traits I needed to rein-corporate into my life to make me complete, to make me whole.

She showed me that I wanted to be the one to make decisions for myself. I wanted to be the one to decide what I had in life and who I allowed in it.

She helped me regain my voice, my strength, and an expectation of fairness.

I would love to be able to say that my friends and family were support-ive and saw the same things I did and decided to work with me to make things better.

I would love to be able to say that. But, of course, I can't.

People who love to gaslight and manipulate others can't stand it when their mark sees the light. It ruins their plans of blaming everyone else but themselves for their own situations. It ruins their good-guy image, which is only that—a mere image, not reality—as they project their negativity onto others around them.

Those people don't suddenly change their ways, so the best course of action is often elimi-nating as much contact with them as possible from your life.

Growing and moving on takes a lot of acceptance. Ac-cepting that we cannot change

> **People who love to gaslight and manipulate others can't stand it when their mark sees the light. It ruins their plans of blaming everyone else but themselves for their own situations.... Those people don't suddenly change their ways, so the best course of action is often eliminating as much contact with them as possible from your life.**

others but only ourselves, our actions, and how we respond is often an extremely difficult lesson to learn. Accepting that we cannot change others and letting them go is often far more emotionally healthy than accepting their poor treatment.

Needless to say, I lost connections with many people—connections that should have been cut years earlier and that had sometimes been the cause of joy but had more and more often been the cause of pain. The day my longtime best friend unfriended me and my entire family on Facebook because I kept a promise to my family and didn't run immediately to her aid was a huge eye-opener. Though ending this relationship was not my choice, it was the catalyst I needed to see how badly I had been used and to finally put my foot down and say "no more" to others who treated me in the same manner. I had tolerated that treatment for far too long.

I know there are many people, often women, who need to take this same step—to cut the connections that bring them down. When women do this and stand up for themselves and say they are done with this treatment, they are often seen as selfish. But it is never selfish to take care of yourself. You are the most important person to you, and don't let anyone tell you otherwise.

These changes have brought an incredible peace to my life—a peace that comes from within me, not from my environment. I know I am better off. Learning to set boundaries has been challenging but rewarding.

Late Bloomer

My life would not be the same if Blodeuwedd had not reached out to me. I would still be stuck in the same old miserable pattern that always ended in pain and disappointment. She showed me that my life has value on its own and I should be treated with respect by those I allow into it. She showed me that I had the strength to break the cycle and the chains that were holding me back.

Finding this connection with the Maiden has done more than make me feel complete; it has brought with it a regeneration of my life's energy. Not only do I feel younger again, but I feel more alive. I have felt a surge in energy, both physical and mental. I adjusted my diet and began a new exercise regime that has helped me learn to appreciate my own body while losing weight and toning muscles I forgot I had. I am the healthiest I have been in fifteen years. When it all comes together, it really all comes together!

There were some subtle changes too. As far back as I could remember, I could not stand the smell of roses, even though they had been one of my biological mother's favorite flowers. The smell literally made me sick to my stomach. Once I began working with Blodeuwedd, that aversion went away and now I enjoy the scent of rose.

While I've had some incredibly terrible experiences along the way, my life finally feels like it is back on track. It took those negative experiences to bring me to the positivity I have today. I have successfully incorporated aspects of the Maiden, Mother, and Crone into myself, and I love the completeness I now feel.

Incorporating (or reincorporating) the Maiden into your life during Cronehood is invigorating and gives you a whole new outlook on

> **Finding this connection with the Maiden has done more than make me feel complete; it has brought with it a regeneration of my life's energy. Not only do I feel younger again, but I feel more alive. I have felt a surge in energy, both physical and mental.**

and appreciation for the status of the Crone as well as the Maiden. The Maiden represents many characteristics that present-day society tells us "old" women shouldn't be, such as energetic, spontaneous, mischievous, sexy, playful, and bold. There is no reason we can't be all of these things, unless we allow others to put restrictions on us. The old "act your age" not only is outdated but can be downright depressing! Who decided how we must act at a certain age? Who decided that gaining years and knowledge and wisdom should somehow knock out the traits we are told to give up as we age?

I love the connection I've found with the Maiden, and with Blodeuwedd in particular. She sent me off in search of my younger self and then helped me incorporate her into my daily life, creating a calmer, more peaceful present and the potential for a bright future.

Meditation to Connect (or Reconnect) with the Maiden

You can perform this working either as a stand-alone meditation or as a meditation in a self-constructed ritual, whichever works best for your practice. Prepare your meditation/ritual area with any supplies, decorations, or comforts you need.

In a meditative state, allow yourself to be at one with the universe. Open your mind to any and all possibilities.

Think back to your younger days—as a child, a teenager, a young person in your twenties. What memories come to mind first? What moments defined who you were? Spend as much time as you need here reminiscing.

When you are ready, ask for a Maiden goddess to join you. Do not ask for a specific goddess. (If you work with a specific pantheon, you may focus on calling a Maiden from it, but don't feel you have to limit yourself to one pantheon only. There may be something to learn from a goddess outside your normal sphere.)

When she arrives, take mental note of who she is. Is this a goddess you have worked with before? Is she new to you? Are you familiar with her history? (If you are not familiar with her, then after you finish the meditation session, be sure to follow up with research about who she is. You will want to repeat this meditation several times, so build up your knowledge base for your next meeting. Whatever goddess comes to you, you will be spending several sessions working with her. She has a message for you. Your job is to listen to what it is and make the recommended changes she shows you.)

Allow the Maiden to introduce herself, then introduce yourself to her. What do you want her to know about you? What do the two of you have in common? What are your differences?

Listen to what she tells you. See yourself through her eyes. What part of yourself does she see that you put away because you were told to or because you believed you had to? Spend plenty of time in this meditation to be sure you get her message. When you are ready to end your session, be sure to thank the Maiden for her presence and guidance.

After your session, journal about your experience. Do you see what your Maiden goddess wanted you to know? What changes can you make to more fully incorporate the Maiden into your daily life?

Repeat this meditation as many times as you feel is necessary. It may easily take several sessions to discover everything you need to. Your Maiden won't give you more than you can handle at any one time, so you can work on different aspects as you go. Don't expect a whole laundry list in one session. Change takes time. Incorporating new aspects and eliminating old habits takes time.

You may even find you are granted an audience with several different Maiden goddesses through your workings. Each one will come to you for a reason. They may all have a different lesson for you, or perhaps different ones will appear if you are not receiving the messages sent by others.

．．．．．．．．．．．．．

Facing our true selves can be terrifying, but know that when working with a goddess to help you through the process, you couldn't have a better teacher or companion to guide you.

Find what is missing in your life. Find what makes you complete and at peace with yourself. We are complicated beings, and as we travel through life, we do leave some pieces of ourselves behind. We do not have to leave all of them, though. Finding what we need to make us whole is the ultimate spiritual goal.

Kerri Connor *has been practicing her craft for over thirty years and runs an eclectic family group called the Gathering Grove. She is a frequent contributor to the Llewellyn annuals and is the author of* Spells for Tough Times: Crafting Hope When Faced With Life's Thorniest Challenges *as well as the upcoming* Wake, Bake & Meditate: Take Your Spiritual Practice to a Higher Level with Cannabis *and* Wake, Bake & Meditate: 420 Daily Meditations. *Kerri resides in northern Illinois.*

Illustrator: Rik Olson

A New Look at the Energies of the Cycle of the Year

Barbara Ardinger

Like the believers of nearly any religion, we Pagans follow the ways given to us by our elders. We have good books, old rituals, and what I call the Received Astronomical Wisdom that say the four seasons officially begin on the solstices and equinoxes. But do they, really? We know the energies of the seasons of our lives tend to rise and fall. So do the energies of the year, and just following along with what everyone else says but not thinking about what's really happening can make those energies seem thinner and less…well, *energetic.*

Perhaps we and our energy levels need to be refreshed as we move through the year. Let's take a new look at the energies of the yearly cycle. As you do so, take a few minutes to examine how the yearly energies reverberate in you. How open to energy are you? How do you receive and express the energies of the year?

The Received Common Wisdom

We know from scholarship based on work at the ancient celestial calendars like Stonehenge and other stone circles and monuments around the world that the Neolithic peoples (and maybe earlier peoples, too) already knew about the solstices and equinoxes. *Solstice* means "sun stands still," i.e., twice a year the sun seems to rise and set in approximately the same place on the horizon. We also know that some of the stone circles and underground monuments were constructed so that on the winter or summer solstice, the sun is seen (as at Stonehenge) to rise over a particular stone or (at the passage grave called Newgrange) to shine through the entrance and illuminate a triple spiral carved into the wall at the end of the passage. *Equinox* means "equal night." Twice a year and equidistant from the solstices, the days and nights are very close to the same length. For eons, farmers have used the solstices and equinoxes to signal planting and harvesting and other significant events and festivals. Take some time now to consider what the solstices and equinoxes mean to you today.

We Pagans celebrate our four major sabbats on the solstices and equinoxes, to which we have added the four cross-quarter days: Imbolc, Beltane, Lammas, and Samhain. You may use other names for these holidays, but the dates are basically the same: February 1–2 (Imbolc), May 1–2 (Beltane), August 1–2 (Lammas), and October 31–November 1 (Samhain). Most of us have special rituals for all eight of the holy days of the cycle of the year, and many of us believe that it's the ritual energy projected by magic circles around the world that helps keep that yearly cycle turning.

The common wisdom since at least the Stone Age is that the seasons begin with the solstices (winter, summer) and equinoxes (spring, fall). That's what the people on TV and the internet say, too. But what if the solstices and equinoxes are actually where the energies of the seasons reach their highest level? Where the energy of one season turns a corner and begins sliding into the energy of the next season? As an analogy, visualize a roof, where the ridge is the sabbat. What went up pauses for a minute on the topmost point, then moves down. Or see the sabbat as the hinge on a door (the seasonal energy) that closes on one room and opens to the next. Ridge and hinge don't stop the energy; they pause it, move it, and redirect it. We walk though the door and we're somewhere else. In sabbat rituals, we feel and magically use the energy, then we move into the next energy.

Seeing How the Energies Really Work

How does winter's energy move? If you live in the Northern Hemisphere, pay attention to what you're seeing in November. (If you live south of the equator, you already know how to reverse what we northerners do.) Take note of how nature has begun to fall asleep in October and November: trees are dropping their leaves and our gardens have begun their long rest, bare above the ground, roots sleeping under the soil, maybe dreaming about rebirth in the spring. We're feeling a bit lazy ourselves, but we keep going. This is the beginning of the metaphorical long winter's nap.

And when in winter are people the liveliest? Look around again. We wake up at the solstice! That's when we're busiest and most active. Is it because of this strong solstice energy that both Hanukkah and Christmas are celebrated near the solstice? Is this why the Norse used the word Yule, which means "mid-winter," to name their holiday? Is

this why Jesus's birthday was moved back from January (possibly his real birth date) to December 25, which is also the birthday of Mithras?

Let's look with our best and clearest vision. If winter peaks at the solstice, then when does the season actually begin? I propose that it's when we know for sure that winter's night is falling: the end of October and the first of November. The standard calendar calls this time Hallowe'en (Hallows Evening, October 31), which is followed in the Christian tradition by All Saints' Day (November 1) and All Souls' Day (November 2). I believe these three holidays—holy days—tell us that winter's energy actually begins to rise at the sabbat we call Samhain. It's the true beginning of winter. After the solstice, of course, all the good wintry energy begins its flow toward the next season.

If winter peaks at the solstice, then when does the season actually begin? I propose that it's when we know for sure that winter's night is falling: the end of October and the first of November.... I believe...that winter's energy actually begins to rise at the sabbat we call Samhain.

Which is springtime. Let's look again with our best and clearest vision. When are we sure the light is returning? When do the hibernating animals creep out of their caves and holes and stretch in the sunshine? When do certain well-meaning people pester defenseless little groundhogs to get a weather forecast? These things are happening when we're celebrating the triple goddess Brigid, who (like some other goddesses) became a saint. Brigid's holy day is February 2. This is when we celebrate the sabbat we call Candlemas or Brigid's Day or Imbolc or

Oimelc, these last two being ancient Celtic terms referring to the breeding of livestock. (Imbolc means "in the belly.") We begin celebrating the return of the light we can now see in plain sight.

Spring's energy builds to mid-spring, the equinox. The nights are getting shorter, and after March 20–21, the days are obviously longer, giving us more time to do whatever we need to do. The energy of spring peaks and now begins to flow into summer.

Which the astronomers tell us begins on June 20–21. But now that we're looking at the seasons with our best and clearest vision, we can see that, yes, the energy has changed. But the change actually began on May 1, Beltane, when mythology and some folk customs tell us that ancient kings "mated" with the earth…or at least with fertile queens. There are interesting myths and legends about how the health and energy of the land are tied to the health and energy of the land's king, who did it out in the fields so the whole kingdom would become more fertile, which is necessary and appropriate in the summer.

Summer's energy begins with planting (those kings were "planting" the fields) in early May and peaks with blossoming in late June. Everything that can bloom is blooming, the crops on the farms are thriving, the bees are buzzing, the fireflies are blinking, and every other insect and animal we can see or think of is active. Young animals born in the spring are now independent, and many of them no longer depend on their mother's milk. School's been out for a few weeks and the kids are reenergized and running around, too. The summer solstice is straight across the year from the winter solstice, that other busiest time of the year. If we look clearly at the energies, we can see that summer actually began at Beltane and reaches its greatest strength at mid-summer, June 20–21, after which the energy begins to flow toward autumn.

The next cross-quarter day is Lammas, August 1–2, also called Lughnasadh or Lughnasa, after the Celtic god Lugh, a sun king who organized festivities to honor his mother, who is sometimes called the

Grain Mother. The old farmers said this was the first harvest, and many of them saved the first stalk of grain from the first harvest to use magically in the second and third harvests. We, too, consider Lammas to be our first harvest, the time when we gather in the "crops" we "sowed" either metaphorically or literally with our spellwork. As August opens, it's still too hot and the sun is bright (sometimes too bright), but when we look with our best and clearest vision, we can see that the days are becoming measurably shorter. Lugh's high energy is beginning to fade. Summer is about over, and we know autumn is just around the corner. In our mundane lives, we're doing our annual shopping for school supplies and getting ready for our own quieter time with the kids out of the house. Autumn is beginning, and its energy will build until the fall equinox on September 21–22.

We can feel the change in the energy—in the air, in our feelings, in the behaviors of insects and animals—at mid-autumn. Nowadays, the fall equinox is sometimes called Mabon, the name of a Welsh god who seems to be falling asleep. The fall equinox is also our second harvest, again either metaphorical or literal. After September 21 or thereabouts, the energy of the annual cycle is obviously moving toward the dark season.

And winter begins on the fourth cross-quarter day: Samhain ("summer's end" to the old Celts) or Hallows. It's the celebration of the beginning of the "dark half of the year," our final harvest, the night when we perhaps do a fireless ritual (no lit candles on the altar). This sabbat has, alas, been demeaned and desecrated by the anti-Pagan, fundamentalist culture with its horror events at theme parks, awful movies, trick-or-treating (which has become all treats and no tricks), and everyone dressed up as ghosts, goblins, werewolves, and superheroes…but scant mention is made of Witches. We Pagans can—and *should*—ignore all that popular nonsense and see Samhain for what it really is: the holy day that ends the year. Nothing to be afraid of. We simply follow the yearly energy into the sacred, healing darkness…and soon we're back where we started: at the winter solstice, where winter's energy is strongest and things start to get moving again.

Here is the revised schedule of the cycle of the year that I propose:

Season	Beginning Sabbat/ Date	Energy Peak
Winter	Samhain (Oct. 31–Nov. 1)	Solstice: Yule, Midwinter
Spring	Imbolc (February 1–2)	Equinox: Ostara, Easter
Summer	Beltane (May 1–2)	Solstice: Litha, Midsummer
Autumn	Lammas (August 1–2)	Equinox: Mabon, Fall

An important note: To be sure, in our mundane lives, we don't have to ignore society's long-held customs. We can smile and nod when people say the seasons begin on the solstices and equinoxes. We can attend to our mundane work in the "real world." But in our spiritual lives, let's pay attention to the true rising and falling energies of the cycle of the year and celebrate them.

I have been running my life according to this revised calendar for many years as I have learned to feel and understand the rising energy of the cross-quarter days that begin the seasons. I've also come to feel when the strongest energies of the seasons occur, and I've planned my personal rituals around the energies I feel. I use appropriate colors (candles, magical tools, altar decorations, my clothing) in the rituals that begin the seasons and black or white for the solstices and equinoxes. Try it yourself. What works for me may not work for you, but what else do we Pagans do if not experiment as we create our personal rituals? Try out different colors, cast your circle facing a different direction, find appropriate poetry to read, or do a good healing dance to get yourself moving. There are many ways to celebrate our spiritual and magical year. And let's remember what Portia says near the end of Shakespeare's *Merchant of Venice*:

> How many things by season seasoned are
> To their right praise and true perfection!

Barbara Ardinger, PhD (*www.barbaraardinger.com*), *is the author of eight books, including* Secret Lives, *a novel about crones and other magical folks, and* Pagan Every Day, *a unique daybook of daily meditations. Her other books include* Goddess Meditations (*the first-ever book of meditations focusing on goddesses*) *and* Finding New Goddesses (*a parody of goddess encyclopedias*). *Her blogs and/or stories appear every month on the website* Feminism & Religion, *http://feminismandreligion.com/, where she is a regular Pagan contributor. She has been writing for the Llewellyn annuals since 2004, and her work has also been published in devotionals to Isis, Athena, and Brigid. Barbara's day job is freelance editing for people who have good ideas for books but don't want to embarrass themselves in print. To date, she has edited more than 300 books, both fiction and nonfiction, on a wide range of topics. She lives in Long Beach, California, with her two rescued cats, Schroedinger and Heisenberg. Her doctorate is in English.*

Illustrator: M. Kathryn Thompson

Magical Self-Care

Nurture Your Body, Mind & Spirit

Reframing & Redirecting Negativity

Autumn Damiana

This is the story of how I learned to effectively deal with negativity as a Witch. It starts about five years ago when I was trying to lose weight. At that time, I had a lot of challenges to overcome. I was getting older, I had low thyroid, and I was taking antidepressants. I tried *everything*. Like any Witch, I used magic to enhance my efforts. Originally I used banishing spells—banish weight, banish hunger, banish low motivation, etc.—but nothing happened. It was only when I finally tried positive magic to help with my weight loss that I succeeded.

It may sound like a weird thing to say to another Witch—to give up banishing spells—especially if you've had good luck with them. However, I truly believe that you will get even better results by focusing on the positive instead. Let me explain.

The Experience That Started It All

Professionally, I work with children. We use the positive reinforcement model of discipline. This includes rewarding children for positive behavior, not dwelling on the negative, and making your expectations clear. When you want a child to walk, you never say, "Please don't run," because the child may then hop or skip. You tell them, "Use your walking feet," so that it is clear what you expect and what is acceptable (and therefore positive) behavior. Saying "don't do such-and-such" does not deter undesirable conduct; it only leaves a hollow of expectation, where the child has to guess what is supposed to happen. It gets even more complicated when dealing with very young children. They have shorter attention spans and their language skills are not fully developed. So when you say to them, "Please don't run," they get confused by the "please don't" part and may focus on the word "run," which is the last word they heard, and therefore they do that.

These ideas resonate with me in terms of magic and spell casting. "Banishing" things only programs magical power to get rid of something, leaving an emptiness to be filled up with…what? And you can't effectively do a banishing and attracting spell at the same time, so why not just do the attracting? Positivity will automatically banish negativity. Also, the subconscious is just like a young child—it is highly suggestible and receptive to whatever you think or say. So you may state, "I want to banish poverty," but your subconscious seizes on the word "poverty" and all of the meaning that goes with it, and your spell does nothing.

Another method is to redirect the negativity. Again, I see this all the time working with children. If a child is throwing blocks inside, instead of scolding them, take the child outside and show them how to throw a ball instead. The child now has a positive outlet for the behavior, which was not theoretically "wrong" but just not appropriate in that situation. You explain to the child why throwing a ball outside instead of blocks inside is better: the ball is made for throwing, it won't hurt anyone, other children will want to play ball with you, etc.

These are all lessons I learned as a teacher about how I can be more effective as a Witch and magical practitioner. This strategy can be summed up by the I Ching, which states that "the best way to fight evil is to make energetic progress in the good." For a Witch, understanding how the conscious and unconscious work together to effect change through magic is one of the greatest lessons that we all must learn, and this includes handling negativity.

Neutralize It

Some years ago there was a proposition on the California ballot that I strongly supported. One day at a busy intersection, I drove by a man holding a sign showing he was against it. I made a huge display of honking my horn and making rude gestures at him. He humbly bowed his head and waved at me, and I immediately felt embarrassed by my behavior. We were on opposing sides of an issue, but he was handling it gracefully and I was not.

Sometimes we manufacture our own negativity. Road rage is a perfect example. Where I live, traffic is ridiculous, and I get upset at people all the time—but I'm in my car where they can't hear me, so who cares, right? The problem is that thoughts, words, and emotions have energy and can affect other people, but they can hurt you, too. You should try to curb your behavior, but sometimes these things slip out, especially out of habit. Therefore, I have developed some strategies to counteract these negative emotions when they come up so that I am not inadvertently wishing harm on another person or carrying around all that negativity with me.

For example, if I yell, "Get out of my way!" I try to remember to add a positive statement, like "And may you have a safe journey." If I swear at someone, I immediately recite this rhyme: "Curses from my lips did fall, which I recant for the good of all." Sometimes I cross myself: I make an X over my body by moving my hand from one shoulder to the opposite hip and then repeating on the other side. This cancels out the anger or other bad feelings I was projecting.

Try forgiveness and understanding. If someone is driving way too fast, consider that maybe it's because they are in a hurry to get to a bathroom.... We all make mistakes, but at the same time, we jump to conclusions that other people are doing harmful things to us on purpose— even though they probably aren't.

Another approach is to try forgiveness and understanding. If someone is driving way too fast, consider that maybe it's because they are in a hurry to get to a bathroom. If someone cuts you off, it could be that they are very distracted by their children arguing in the car. We all make mistakes, but at the same time, we jump to conclusions that other people are doing harmful things to us on purpose—even though they probably aren't. The same is true in all aspects of life. Sometimes bad things just happen. It's what you do in these situations that counts.

Positive Affirmations

I used to be so skeptical of positive affirmations, like when Witches say "Love and Light." I thought it sounded like a bunch of New Age nonsense. Although the more trite representations of this highly effective tool can put people off, the reality is that positive affirmations can really change your life. You don't have to use the ones that other people recommend, and in fact you probably shouldn't. It's important to find what works best for you.

Here are some affirmations that I have written, which I hope will inspire you to write your own.

• Elemental connection to the universe:

I am water and light, stardust and stone, spirit and breath, beauty and love.

• A good way to start the day:

I wake with purpose. I walk with faith. I speak with truth. I act with love.

• Statement of self-love and purpose:

My needs and wants are real. I tend to them as I would a garden— with patience, attention, and devotion. In time they cannot help but bloom into reality.

• Devotional to the God/Goddess (or any other deity):

Wherever I go, you are there,
From my heart's content to the depths of despair.
I heed you when I feel your call.
I will forever be in your thrall.
Show me my path, which you help decide.
I trust you completely to be my guide.

Here is an example of how you can write affirmations that are more goal-oriented. I had a so-called friend who turned on me quite suddenly, and she never explained why, nor did she want to acknowledge or talk about it. So frustrating! I had a hard time facing her after that, so I wrote this to help me through:

I *will bark, but I won't bite.*
I *will hover, but I won't sting.*
I *will stand, but I won't fight.*
I *will find* _____ *in all things.*

This is a great set of affirmations to use when you don't want to make things worse but you don't want to look or feel weak by backing down either. The word I used here to fill in the blank was "kindness," because when I was angry I wanted to "kill her with kindness," which, honestly, made the affirmation kind of a joke.

But here is the really amazing thing. Even a half-assed willingness to change on my part was transformed by repeating these affirmations. You can't say "I will find kindness in all things" over and over without it actually happening, whether you like it or not!

At first I used kindness to forgive myself for not dealing well with the situation emotionally. Then I found the kindness to forgive her, because there may have been some stressors in her life that had made her act that way. And then finally I remembered to see the kindness *in* her that had made me want to be friends with her in the first place. This is when I found peace with the situation, realizing that she was not a bad person just because she no longer valued our friendship! I took the negativity she threw at me and redirected it into a positive life lesson.

You can use the same affirmation with any positive word, like "love" or "acceptance" or even "truth," and if you use it over time to work through an issue, you will find a similar resolution.

Science and Magic Together

Cognitive behavioral therapy, dialectical behavioral therapy, and mindfulness therapy are some of the most common methods that psychologists use to help patients retrain their brains to reject negative thoughts and behavior. Some of the techniques from these therapies are very popular, and you may have heard about them already. Here are three spells that work with such techniques so you can get the maximum benefit from both science and magic.

SMILE LIKE MONA LISA

Whenever you feel yourself sinking into anxiety or depression, this is a simple way to help yourself cope until you can employ stronger self-help methods. Simply find a mirror and gaze into it, looking at yourself as if you were a stranger, without emotion or judgment. Then recite this charm three times:

> *My mood is light, I reject the belief*
> *That these bad thoughts will weigh me down.*
> *Now I only feel relief*
> *And choose to smile instead of frown.*

While you are speaking, smile a half-smile, like Mona Lisa. Studies show that by mimicking the physical attributes of happiness, like smiling, you can actually trick your body into feeling happier. Don't try for a big toothy grin, as this will only make your face hurt, but practice the half-smile and you will feel a lot better. After speaking the incantation in the mirror, keep smiling for at least ten minutes or more while you go about your daily life!

Pick a rubber band that is special to you because of its color or some other association. Safely light a yellow candle. Watch the funniest thing you can think of: a movie, TV show, stand-up comedy routine, etc. Hold the rubber band in your dominant hand, and when you notice yourself smiling big or laughing, project that happy feeling into the band. When you are done watching, carefully pass the rubber band over the candle a few times while saying these words:

Warmth of mirth and warmth of smile,
You'll be with me all the while.
Unhappiness will turn to glee,
And only laughter will stay with me.

Put the rubber band on your non-dominant hand. Snap it against your wrist whenever you feel a negative thought, which will shock your body out of that thinking for a moment. Then immediately follow it up with something funny or silly—do a little dance, or say to yourself, "Aww, snap!" or "No, you didn't!" or whatever else will amuse you and make you laugh. In time, you will stop thinking as negatively and will find the humor in the situation instead.

> **Snap [the rubber band] against your wrist whenever you feel a negative thought…Then immediately follow it up with something funny…In time, you will stop thinking as negatively and will find the humor in the situation instead.**

We're all guilty of negative self-talk, because we all occasionally feel like we're just not good enough on some level. This is normal, but when these negative messages take over and start interfering with our daily lives, things can get out of hand. When that happens, grab a large piece of paper (binder paper is fine) and fold it in half. On the left side, list all the negative thoughts you have. On the right side, write a positive statement that contradicts each negative one, then scribble out the negative thought. Use "I" statements to make it personal.

Here is a short sample list:

Negative	Positive
I'm ugly.	I have a happy, kind face.
I'm a loser.	I'm good at lots of things.
I'm an underachiever.	I get good grades in school.
I'm not likable.	I have lots of good friends.

When you've made your list, split the paper down the middle. Tear the side with the negative thoughts into shreds. Wad these up into a ball. Then take the piece of paper with the positive thoughts and wrap it around the ball—you are overpowering the negative with the positive. Tie this up in a scrap of fabric with a piece of ribbon or string, or place it in a mojo bag. Keep it with you until you begin to feel better about yourself. When you do, unwrap the fabric and either throw away the paper or burn it.

Emergency Measures

Most Witches worry about being hexed at some time or another, and while this doesn't usually happen, we may still get bombarded with negative energy from a variety of sources (such as family, job, bad luck, or even ourselves!), and it can feel like we are being attacked. Here are some fast-acting magical strategies to use in these types of situations.

Have a Magical Meal

Carve words into a potato that combat the negativity you are experiencing—"good luck" or "good health," for example. Bake the potato, and visualize the heat searing that intention into it as the skin begins to crisp. Finally, prepare the potato as you like and then eat it, skin and all, to manifest the magic. This spell can also be done with other baked/roasted vegetables and fruits, like carrots or apples.

Make a Positive Potion

Mix ¼ cup water with ¼ teaspoon salt, then spit in it. Stir with a bay leaf until the salt is dissolved. Use your finger to anoint each of the windows and doors in your house, and make sure to add a dab to each of the walls. Speak this incantation as you work:

For me and mine, I mark this place, and only good may fill this space.

Work with Crystals

Sit in a comfortable position holding a crystal cluster or polished sphere, as these will radiate energy in all directions. Visualize that you are inside a bubble of light that is the same color as the crystal. Let the color fill the bubble, surrounding and infusing you with its energy. Imagine negativity sent your way as arrows, which bounce off the bubble and fall harmlessly to the ground, where they are absorbed by the earth and disappear. Use amethyst for peace and calm, citrine for happiness, hematite for grounding, rose quartz for love and forgiveness, tiger's eye for courage, etc.

Do a Little Banishing Magic to Clear Out Any Bad Vibes

As a last resort, you can burn sage or palo santo, sprinkle salt water, use defensive crystals such as smoky quartz or black tourmaline, or take a ritual cleansing bath. Be sure to perform an attraction spell afterward to fill the void you just created with positive intent!

Autumn Damiana *is an author, artist, crafter, and amateur photographer. She is a solitary eclectic Cottage Witch who has been following her Pagan path for almost two decades and is a regular contributor to the Llewellyn annuals. Along with writing and making art, Autumn has a degree in early childhood education and is currently pursuing further studies. She lives with her husband and doggie familiar in the beautiful San Francisco Bay Area. Visit her online at autumndamiana.com.*

Illustrator: Tim Foley

Grounding & Earthing Techniques

Cerridwen Iris Shea

One of the wonderful aspects of an evolving spiritual practice is the ability to learn new techniques and develop new ideas, and apply them moving forward. A variety of skills creates options, so you can use what works best in any given situation.

I was lucky enough to train with a traditional coven. It gave me a solid foundation for my work (which I often didn't appreciate enough at the time), and gave me the tools to evolve my own practices. Although the coven is no longer together (two of our members died; the rest of us are scattered throughout the world), I often find myself going back to the basics I learned there and building on them.

I trained in an urban environment. I now live in a more rural one, and have adapted what I learned to fit my landscape, both physical and emotional. I ground before any magical work or circle casting, and I ground after any magical working (or else I get a headache or feel out-of-sorts for days after). I use grounding techniques after a stressful day, or when someone else tries to catch me in their emotional maelstrom. Grounding works with the shielding I do on any given day when I'm out in chaos. I don't need to cast a circle for every grounding, but I need to ground before and after every circle.

Why Ground Before *and* After the Work?

The strength of emotion and will in your magical work affects the outcome. Strong emotion and will are important, but so is the need to be calm and focused. The combination of "calm" and "emotion" might seem like a contradiction, but it's not. The desire and the need must be strong, and the working needs to be well thought out, along with the possible consequences. The emotion in the work is real but also focused and controlled. Flinging out a spell in a fit of pique or lashing out angrily with magic instead of taking a step back and looking at the best way to handle a conflict will come back to haunt you. Grounding before a working helps with the focus and with the ability to raise energy. If you haven't thought things through, grounding before a working can bring clarity that gives you the opportunity to change course before performing a poorly thought-out ritual, and prevents mistakes that can backfire.

Grounding after the work prevents a buildup of excess energy that can lead to headache, grouchiness, poor sleep, and general dis-ease.

Basic Grounding Technique

This is the most basic grounding technique I learned. I prefer to do this after the working but before I open the circle. I kneel and place my palms on the floor or the ground. I visualize any excess energy flowing back into the ground, to be recycled as Gaia sees fit. When I lived in a city, I imagined the energy flowing down through the support beams of the building and back into the ground. Stop when you feel quiet and balanced. Don't push all your own energy out and drain yourself. The goal is to release excess energy, not all energy.

Before a working, I ground with a variation of Tadasana, or Mountain Pose, from my yoga practice. I stand straight, with my feet flat on the ground, aligning shoulders, hips, knees, and heels. Hands are relaxed at my sides. I follow my breath. I feel the ground steady and firm beneath my feet. I feel supported, calm, and confident. Only when I feel all three do I move on to cast the circle and perform the ritual.

Basic Earthing Technique

I do this in my back yard after a stressful day. I stand barefoot in the grass. I let all the stress flow out of me through my feet and into the ground. I do this until I feel calm and relaxed.

You can create a similar result by sitting on rocks or on a wooden or stone bench (genuine stone or wood, not concrete or pressboard). Sit on the bench. Imagine the stress flowing out of your body, through the bench, and down into the earth. You don't want to leave the negative energy in the bench, or the next person who sits down might absorb it. You want to make sure it goes all the way into the earth, to be recycled into positive energy.

Metal has a different energy. A metal bench has a different type of flow. I find metal better for energizing than for calming.

Full-Body Earthing Technique

If I've had an exceptionally stressful day, I'll lie down on the grass. I'll let the stress flow out of my body, not just from my feet but from any part of my body that is touching the ground. Yes, you can do this on a blanket, towel, or yoga mat (especially if you're doing this in a public park).

Grounding Stones

I have several stones that I use for grounding. One is from a beach and one is from a forest. Hematite is another favorite. I use hematite for several purposes, but I have one particular hematite just for grounding. Black tourmaline is another good one, as is tiger's eye. I also have something I bought on Martha's Vineyard that was called "dragonstone" in the store. It's actually a green-and-brown-flecked jasper that I use in stressful times. All of these stones were cleansed in my ritual circle and assigned the task of grounding.

Grounding stones are great because you can carry them in a pocket or purse. They're an on-the-go tool. Sometimes it's enough to just reach into your pocket and massage the stone for a few minutes to lessen the stress. Think of the old-fashioned worry stones. They fulfill a similar function.

I cleanse my grounding stones every quarter or so. I don't want the negative energy or stress to build up. I had a stone crack from stress once when I didn't cleanse it for months and was going through a very difficult time. To cleanse, I put the stones

Grounding stones are great because you can carry them in a pocket or purse. They're an on-the-go tool. Sometimes it's enough to just reach into your pocket and massage the stone for a few minutes to lessen the stress.

first in water overnight on a dark moon. (Some stones don't like salt, so for those I use clear water charged with cleansing.) Then, on the following full moon, I put them out in the moonlight overnight.

To charge water, I do the following in daylight, standing in the sun (although it doesn't have to be outside). I take the bowl of water I'll use to soak the stones and I stand in the sun, feeling the connection between the sun (fire), the earth, and the water. I use my breath, adding the elements of air and spirit. This bowl of water has now been touched by the five elements, and I declare (either silently or out loud) that its job is to cleanse the stones. I put the stones in the bowl and place it on my altar for the three-day period of the day before the dark moon, the dark moon, and the first day of the new moon. I then pour the water away, down a drain or into my earthing pot (more on the earthing pot below), then dry the stones and leave them on my altar. On the day before the next full moon, I set the stones on a black or purple cloth. I leave them out in the moonlight for the three-day period of that night, the night of the full moon, and the night after the full moon. During the day, I keep the stones wrapped in the cloth, out of the sunlight. Now they're ready for another quarter of the year.

Stones can also be cleansed by burying them in the ground or a pot of earth for three days. Again, I do this during the three-day period of the day before the dark moon, the dark moon, and the first day of the new moon. Or they can be cleansed with breath, any time you feel it's necessary. Hold the stone in your dominant hand. Inhale deeply. Exhale across the stone, visualizing all the negative energy dissipated and removed.

I usually have at least one grounding stone on my altar, one in my purse, and the others wrapped in cloth, stored in my magical cabinet.

Earth Rebalancing Technique

Both the earthing and the full-body earthing technique can be taken a step further, if you've been feeling scattered or exhausted and need to replenish yourself with some earth energy. In this case, let all the stress drain out until you feel neutral. Now imagine yourself pulling the earth energy up into your body.

This sensation feels different to everyone. It reminds me of how wonderful, calming, and connected it feels when I work in the warm, moist, loamy soil of the garden. There's a sense of warmth, strength, and calm. When I do an earthing or a rebalancing, the sense memory of that feeling is what I use as I pull up the energy.

You'll feel it when you have enough earth energy, when you feel energized. Pull up too much, and you'll feel heavy and weighted. You can always drain some of the energy back into the ground. The more you practice this technique, the more you'll feel what works for you.

You can do this as a walking meditation as well. Have you ever felt overwhelmed and taken a break by taking a walk? Do you find that it clears your head? Moving, connecting to the ground, is revitalizing you. You are actively working the stress out of your body as you walk into the earth, and are replacing it with fresh earth and air energy.

Earthing Pot

When I lived in New York City and had to perform most of my rituals indoors, the earthing pot was one of my most important tools. It was a simple terracotta flowerpot about two-thirds full of potting soil. I cleansed and consecrated it before use, but I kept it on my kitchen windowsill, not my altar. If I needed to bury something from a spell, it went into the pot. If I needed to refresh some crystals, they went into the pot. If I needed to pour out some ritual liquid and the sink wasn't appropriate, it went into the pot. If someone was harassing me

When I lived in New York City and had to perform most of my rituals indoors, the earthing pot was one of my most important tools.... If I needed to bury something from a spell, it went into the pot. If I needed to refresh some crystals, they went into the pot.... The intent was that whatever was put into the pot would lose its negativity and be turned into positivity.

(happens a lot when you're a single woman in Manhattan) and I wanted something stronger than putting the person's name in ice in my freezer, I would write The intent was always that whatever was put into the pot would lose its negativity and be turned into positivity the person's name or a description of the person on a piece of rice paper, then tie the paper around a small pebble with natural twine or silk thread and put it in the pot. If I felt disconnected from the earth, and the houseplants or my grounding stones weren't enough and I couldn't get to a park, I would put my hand in the pot for a few minutes.

The intent was that whatever was put into the pot would lose its negativity and be turned into positivity. Twice a year (once before Beltane and once before Samhain), I'd take the pot to a friend's house outside of New York City and, with her permission, empty it into her compost heap. I'd scrub out the pot, refill it with potting soil, then cleanse and consecrate it, and it would be good for another six months.

Sometimes, if I had a struggling seedling, I'd transplant it for a few days into the earthing pot so it could recover. When it was strong enough, I'd put it back into its own pot.

Living in a place where I have a garden, as I do now, I rarely use an earthing pot. My entire garden can serve that function when necessary. Sometimes I use a small earthing pot (which I keep on the deck) for a short-term spell for prosperity or protection. But most of the time I make use of the entire garden. I use a combination of feng shui, cardinal directions, sun and shade, and the unexpected plants that "volunteer" to grow in a particular spot. In fact, some of them are determined to grow there, no matter how often I move or remove them, seeded by birds or other wildlife in the yard. Once I understand what the plant is and why it is determined to grow there, I can use it in my magical work. But when I lived on the eighth floor of a New York City apartment, the earthing pot was a vital part of my practice.

. . . .

Meditation and yoga practices have added to my understanding of how grounding and earthing techniques help me create an overall more holistic life. My experiences in classes and workshops, as well as out in the garden, encourage me to keep trying new things. Detailed notes, with dates, moon phases, retrogrades, and weather, help me see patterns and make adjustments. There's nothing like the resonance of feeling like "maybe I'll try this, because I feel like I need a bit more earth energy" and working with it until you feel unified—and then experiencing how it improves your life.

So go on and play in the dirt!

Cerridwen Iris Shea *was an urban witch and is now a coastal witch who focuses on kitchen, hearth, garden, and sea magic. She wrote for Llewellyn for sixteen years, took a break, and is delighted to be back. Visit her at her website,* Cerridwen's Cottage, *www.cerridwenscottage.com, and her blog,* Kemmyrk, *https://kemmyrk.wordpress.com.*

Illustrator: Rik Olson

Fear, Creativity & Spiders: Working with Arachne

Raechel Henderson

My previous workshop was a converted garage. It was unheated, uninsulated, and riddled with hidey-holes and cracks. The walls were lined with shelves overloaded with bolts of fabric, patterns, thread, sewing tools and baskets, sewing machines, books, and boxes of finished and half-finished projects. All of this added to the hodgepodge ambience that I found useful to my creative process. It also played host to a whole ecology of insects, as well as the occasional mouse. As such, I found myself forced into close quarters with various spiders.

Spindly house spiders hung out in the window above my sewing table. Black chitinous ones hid in the darkened corners. Jumping spiders, belying their name, were often found on the ceiling. On occasion one would even scuttle out from under one of the sewing machines, giving me a start. For someone who is totally freaked out by spiders, this was not the most ideal work environment.

Despite my fear, I had work to do. I had spent more than a decade supporting my family with my sewing, so I forced myself each day to head into my workshop, spiders or no. During those first few weeks in the workshop, I learned what corners to avoid. I would give boxes a tap and a jiggle before I took them off the shelf to allow any spider the opportunity to skedaddle. And I became less fearful.

The big black spiders still creeped me out, but the long-legged house spiders spinning webs in the windowsill didn't bother me as much. They were delicate, almost ethereal creatures, and as far from threatening as I could imagine. I could recognize that they were just living their lives and keeping the bug population down. If I left them alone, they would extend the same courtesy to me.

I was also exploring ways to bring my witchcraft practice into my work. I wanted to build a practice that was akin to kitchen witchery but founded on sewing. As I worked at my machines, I played with various ideas: trying to adapt color correspondences to sewing, working out the magickal properties of fabric, and so on. I would stop my work and gaze out the window while my thoughts swirled, trying to fit them together.

It was around this time that I made the connection between those spinning spiders and Arachne.

Depending on who is telling the tale, Arachne was the victim either of a jealous Athena or the realization that her own skills were no match for the goddess. Either way, her fate was the same in all the tales: she was transformed into the first spider, and was inexorably linked with the woven arts for all eternity. As a woman who took up sewing to support my daughter after divorce, I could relate to Arachne's story. There was always a feeling of having to prove myself with each project taken on, with each stitch sewn. Granted, failure on my part wouldn't end with me being turned into a spider. The fact that Arachne was not a deity in the strictest sense made her more relatable to me.

After a while I would find myself talking to Arachne through the spiders. I'd complain about a particularly difficult bit of sewing, or I would brag about a beautiful seam where the stitches were even and well placed. Being a seamstress means a lot of hours working alone, so having someone to talk to is nice sometimes. It was this relationship that helped inform and build my sew craft.

Like the strands of a web, I began to see how my work could be connected to my magickal intentions. Just like a kitchen witch would choose basil and garlic to add loving energies to their spaghetti sauce, I was paying more attention to colors, patterns, and materials.

Like the strands of a web, I began to see how my work could be connected to my magickal intentions. Just like a kitchen witch would choose basil and garlic to add loving energies to their spaghetti sauce, I was paying more attention to colors, patterns, and materials. If I was making items for sale, I started using only pins with green heads. I started adding stitched runes to the inside hems of clothes for loved ones to give them added protection. I would mark runes on my sewing machine when I had a deadline to help me stay focused and stave off doubts that I would finish in time. And each day I would look at Arachne, sitting and spinning in the windowsill, and know that I was weaving my own magick.

About a year ago I left that workshop behind. My current one is set up in a finished basement that is carpeted and heated. I have yet to see a single mouse (much to the disappointment of the house cats). The spiders, however, are here. Chitinous, jumping, and spindly, they all live in new places. The windows of my workspace are high above and let in little light and no view worth staring at. Even so, Arachne has found places to settle, most often from the undersides of the shelves.

My working relationship with Arachne led to me write a book of sewing magick, *Sew Witchy*, and continues to this day. I walk downstairs, say good morning, and ask, "What are we going to work on today?" The answer is always, "Something magickal."

DIY Fabric Tray

The soft fabric tray project outlined here is a perfect introduction to including magick in your sewing. It is a simple craft, requiring no complicated pattern or sewing techniques. It can be easily resized to whatever dimensions suit your needs, and you end up with a useful item.

This tray takes about an hour to put together. If you can, find a time to sew it during the waxing moon to tap into the energies of growth and change, especially if you'll be using it to hold your runes or tarot cards. Pick fabric prints that tie into your intended use for the tray. For example, use prints that feature crystal balls, tarot cards, or other mystical images for a tray meant to hold your oracle tools. If the tray will be used to hold special jewelry or scents, pick a fabric that is printed with hearts (for self-love), pentagrams (for confidence in your magick), or symbols related to deities you work with (to enhance your connection to them). You can work color magick into your tray through your choice of fabric and thread as well.

While cotton is recommended for this project, it is suitable for a variety of fabrics. You'll be fusing your fabric to the interfacing, which will require an iron with a steam setting. If you choose a delicate or

synthetic fabric, you might want to use a press cloth—simply a piece of muslin that is placed between the iron and the fabric to prevent scorching or melting. Consult the owner's manual of your iron to find out which setting to use when pressing. Heavy fabrics such as velvet, denim, or canvas may need extra pressing and to have their seams trimmed close to the stitching to reduce bulk.

The craft interfacing used in this project is a thick material that gives the tray structure. The interfacing called for is "doubled-sided fusible," meaning it has a layer on each side that melts and fuses with fabric when it comes into contact with heat. You want to make sure you have the double-sided type, so that both the top and the bottom of the tray fuse to the interfacing. It is available from most hobby shops and online.

Tray Instructions

This fabric tray can be used in a variety of ways. Use it to hold your runes or tarot cards when you aren't using them. When you are using them, you can lay them out on the tray in the same way you would place them on a cloth, table, or altar. Or use the tray to hold herbs, crystals, jewelry, or other items. If sewn using the following instructions, the finished tray will measure 6 x 6 inches, with walls that are 1 inch tall.

MATERIALS

- One $7\frac{7}{8}$ x $7\frac{7}{8}$-inch piece of double-sided fusible craft interfacing

- Two 9 x 9-inch squares of fabric

- Thread

- Sewing machine, with regular and heavy-duty needles

- Quilting pen or pencil

- Steam iron

Preparation

1. Cut a 1-inch square from each corner of the interfacing.

Steps

1. Take your two squares of fabric. With right sides together, sew a ½-inch seam around all four sides of the fabric, leaving a 3-inch gap for turning. Use a needle in your machine that is appropriate for the fabric.

2. Clip the corners and trim the seams.

3. Turn the fabric right-side out. Use a skewer or chopstick to push out the corners. Press with an iron.

4. Fold the interfacing into thirds and insert it into the 3-inch opening of the fabric. Unroll the interfacing inside the fabric so it flattens.

5. Press, using steam, to fuse the interfacing to the fabric on both sides.

6. Sew ⅛ inch around all the edges of the tray. Use a heavy-duty needle in your machine so it will go through all the layers.

7. Using a quilting pen or pencil, mark the interior stitching by drawing lines 1¾ inch from the edge of each side. The lines will meet up to form a square in the middle. Stitch this interior square.

8. If you are using a quilting pen that requires heat to fade the lines, then press the tray.

9. To sew the corners, bring two perpendicular sides together to form a triangle. Sew a verticle line 1 inch from the point of the triangle through all the layers. Sew back and forth over this line a couple of times to reinforce the seam. Repeat with the other three corners.

10. If you wish, press your tray along the interior lines to give the folds a crisp finish.

RESIZING INSTRUCTIONS

This tray is easy to customize. Decide how large you want the interior of the tray to be, then decide how deep you want the walls of the tray to be. Add the wall measurement to the interior measurement. Finally, add 1 inch for the seam allowance (giving you a ½-inch seam allowance on each side). For instance, if you want a tray that has an interior of 4 inches and walls that are 1 inch deep, then you'll want to cut two fabric pieces that are 6 x 6 inches: 4" (finished tray measurement) + 1" (wall measurement) + 1" (seam allowance) = 6" (size of each fabric square).

For the inside craft interfacing, you'll cut a square that is 1⅛ inch smaller than your fabric squares. This takes into account the 1 inch lost to the seam allowances. The extra ⅛ inch allows the interfacing to fit without strain, so the edges of the tray won't be wonky. Using the previous example, the interfacing for a 4-inch tray (which uses two 6-inch fabric squares) would be a 4⅞-inch square.

Cut out squares on each corner of the interfacing to match the depth of the walls. Again, using the previous example, you would cut out 1-inch squares on each corner of the interfacing for the corner seams.

Then sew your customized tray as per the instructions.

Raechel Henderson *is a dual class seamstress/shieldmaiden. She has been sewing professionally since 2008 and has traveled around the Midwest region selling her handmade bags, skirts, coats, and accessories at various events and conventions. Arachne hangs out in the window of her workshop, reminding her to check the tension on the sewing machines. She maintains a blog at idiorhythmic.com and is on Instagram and Facebook. You can find more sewing magick in her 2019 book,* Sew Witchy: Tools, Techniques & Projects for Sewing Magick.

Illustrator: M. Kathryn Thompson

Reclaim Your Space

Melanie Marquis

Sometimes I find myself beset with feelings of gloom and doom even when nothing in particular is the matter— at least, nothing that I'm able or willing to easily identify as a direct cause! This is something that happens to all of us. While it's important to acknowledge our emotions and give our feelings space, it's equally important to remember that each of us is the keeper of this space that lies within our heart and mind. Unpleasant feelings that linger for longer than we want them to are like intruders on our private property, and we have every right to serve an eviction notice to these

no-longer-welcomed, emotionally charged energies. Your inner world of body, mind, and spirit is your own personal and private domain, akin to a sacred space or a magick circle.

There are ways to reclaim your inner space, and the most important key to success in achieving this is the desire to do so and the understanding that you do indeed deserve to do so. This article offers some methods to try and some ideas to ponder to help get you started in reclaiming your space both in the short term and for the long term. Don't be afraid or ashamed to also seek professional counseling, therapy, medication, or whatever else might be needed to help you reclaim your inner space.

You Are the Circle, the Cauldron, and the Cup

A useful analogy is to consider your inner world as your own sacred space of sorts. You might think of it as the magick circle cast within a room or an outdoor space before a magickal ritual begins, a space that is made by pushing out from the area anything unwanted—such as doubts, fear, and negativity—and inviting in only what is wanted and welcome—sustaining forces, nurturing forces, and forces that have your own best interest at heart.

Just as you can command and direct energies within an external magick circle, you have within you the power and the inherent right to guide and command the energies within your own internal sacred space. You might also connect with the analogy of seeing your soul as akin to the magick cup: the witch's symbol of the Goddess and her cauldron, the cosmic womb from which everything emerges and to which all will return in a never-ending cycle of life and rebirth. The place where feelings reside within us is like a "holy grail" or cup that can forever be refilled with whatever it is we choose to pour into it. However you look at it, your inner world—your inner being—is your own space. Your body occupies a certain amount of space, and so too does your soul. Give yourself the space and room you need to let your spirit shine at maximum illumination!

Reclaim Your Space in the Short Term

This method can be used to help you shake off unpleasant feelings and shift your emotions in a more positive direction in the present moment. The effects will be temporary, but it's a quick way to jump-start yourself into a better mood or shield yourself from the emotional barbs that others may be slinging at you currently.

Direct your awareness and focus inward, and observe what emotions and thoughts you find there. Just as you would scan a ritual space for unwanted energies when casting a magick circle, take a keen look at the energies and emotions that are currently taking up space within you. Is there anything in your inner space that you would rather not allow to remain there? Take a deep breath and remember your ability to love. Think of something you love until you are able to feel that emotion of loving within your heart. Then, in a series of long and deep breaths, exhale as you imagine that this loving energy is expanding from your heart center to fill your being, driving out and away from your inner space any unpleasant emotions or unwanted energies that you wish to be rid of in the current moment.

After you have driven out as much negative energy as possible, spread your arms out wide, with your open palms facing forward or skyward. Think of the energies and emotions that you would like to be filled with right now, and invite these energies to enter into you. Place your hands over your heart as you take back into yourself the loving power you utilized to drive out the unwanted energies and re-claim your inner space.

Reclaim Your Space for the Long Term

While temporarily banishing an unwanted feeling of gloom from your inner space in the present moment is one thing, reclaiming your inner space for the long term can be a much more difficult and arduous project. We are all works in progress, and processing through long-held trauma and deep-seated feelings of hurt isn't something that can be done instantly through a quickly cast charm or magick spell. This space within our heart and mind gets bombarded with stress, negative beliefs, painful experiences, and other unpleasant emotions throughout our lives, and over time we may realize that these feelings have taken up permanent residence within us. It is up to us to reclaim ownership of this space within us so that we can free ourselves from limiting influences and past traumas and manifest in our lives that which we truly seek.

When we endure painful experiences that cause our soul to experience suffering, we tend to make that part of ourselves smaller and smaller, attempting to hide it away in order to best protect it. While doing so may have served us well in the moment, enabling us to disconnect enough to be able to survive whatever pains we were enduring, we can really get cheated in the long run if we don't remember to liberate these aspects of our soul that we have closed in or shut off.

This space within our heart and mind gets bombarded with stress, negative beliefs, painful experiences, and other unpleasant emotions throughout our lives... It is up to us to reclaim ownership of this space within us so that we can free ourselves from limiting influences and past traumas and manifest in our lives that which we truly seek.

Remember, this space within you is your own space! It is your space to reclaim and to refill with whatever you choose. Thinking of things in these terms can help you to realize on both a conscious and a subconscious level that you really do deserve to feel good, to feel happy, to be nourished and nurtured. The pains you have endured were an abomination. No one, including you, deserves hardships and traumas. You deserve to reclaim your space and to let your soul expand your spirit well beyond the space you currently occupy. This desire to reclaim your inner space, your inner peace—to rid yourself of any lingering effects and restrictions caused by past pains—is the fuel that makes deep healing possible. These painful energies are powerful, and it takes a feeling of righteousness and a desire for justice, the certainty that you are on the right side of things, to conquer and banish these energies for good.

With your heart and your mind on board, the ritual that follows can give you the extra support and transformative power you need to go through the process of reclaiming your inner space for the long term.

Get a piece of paper and a pen, and take an inventory of what you find to be deeply rooted in your inner space. Are there any self-doubting beliefs or self-sabotaging energies that stem from past or current unpleasant or traumatic experiences? Do you truly welcome all the feelings and energies you find within yourself to be there in your sacred space? If you find anything within yourself that you would not want to allow in your home, your magick circle, or your ritual space, write these things down on your piece of paper. When you are finished, read through all you have written. Know that it is your choice what to let go of and what to allow to remain.

If you are ready to begin the process of letting go of the things you have written on your list, shred the paper into tiny pieces and burn the scraps as you think about the ways in which you would like to transform. Repeat this ritual monthly for several months or for as long as it takes. You may wish to time it to coincide with the dark or waning moon. After a while, you will find that you have emerged in a place of healing and inner peace that invites you to make significant and lasting positive changes in your life and in your mindset.

Actualizing the Potential of Your Inner Space

You are a vessel of spirit, a cauldron of soul, a mixing pot of emotion, and with the right ingredients, you can cook up some really good stuff! Just like the witch's magick circle, the sacred space within you is a place for creation, a place where seeds may be planted that will grow into the fruits of love and abundance. If you find that your inner space has been taken over by negative feelings and self-harming beliefs, it's up to you to do whatever it takes to root out these "invasive species" so that the seeds you choose to plant in your life will have the space and nourishment needed to thrive and grow to fruition.

Melanie Marquis *is the creator of the* Modern Spellcaster's Tarot (*illustrated by Scott Murphy*) *and the author of several books, including* A Witch's World of Magick; The Witch's Bag of Tricks; Carl Llewellyn Weschcke: Pioneer and Publisher of Body, Mind & Spirit; Witchy Mama (*with Emily A. Francis*); Beltane; Lughnasadh; *and* Llewellyn's Little Book of Moon Spells. *The founder of United Witches Global Coven and a local coordinator for the Pagan Pride Project, Melanie loves sharing magick with others and has presented workshops and rituals to audiences across the US. She lives in Denver, Colorado.*

Illustrator: Tim Foley

Witch, Heal Thyself

Monica Crosson

I am a Witch who has worked hard to maintain a simple life and escape the bonds of our modern world. My social media accounts are filled with pictures of riverside sabbat celebrations and garden treasures growing amongst an ideal Pacific Northwest backdrop. Setbacks that I may post about probably seem small to most. For example, last spring I was devastated to walk out my back door to find that my free-range donkey had discovered the tasty sweetness of raspberry leaves. One morning I awoke to find she had devoured nine rows, reducing my yield to less than five pounds of the coveted fruit.

I have had people private message me about what a wonderful life I lead. And to those people I always message back, "Yes, my insta-life is pretty nice. It's real life that gets tricky." Because there are things that I will never post on social media. So there's no selfie of me crying in the starkness of my daughter's empty room the week before she moved out—bittersweet tears laced with memories of my little shadow who grew into one of the most amazing human beings and powerful Witches I have been blessed to know. No one saw 3:00 a.m. posts of me at the ER worried about my son when he stopped taking his medication for his bipolar illness or of my inner dialogue blaming myself because the illness runs in my family—hence it is my fault. He is a beautiful soul who has since dedicated his career to helping others who suffer with mental illness, and I couldn't be prouder as a parent.

I didn't take pictures of my breakdown at my writer's group where I ugly-cried all over my carefully typed pages because I was quite certain I was the worst, most unsuccessful writer in the entire world, leaving the other members of the group completely gobsmacked by my outburst. And when my heart was crushed by a relatively recent conversation with my mother, I didn't post one of those clever "I said, they said" posts.

So although my social media is a pretty good picture of my simple day-to-day activities and the portion of my magickal life that I feel comfortable sharing, it doesn't represent the tumultuous battle that is constantly playing out in my head: the roaring insecurity that reminds me that I am not good enough—the echo of childhood trauma that resonates so deeply the memories pound like a drum—and an overactive brain that does not allow for me to focus on anything for any length of time. All of this makes life pretty overwhelming at times.

But a few years ago, something changed in how I dealt with my internal turmoil. I was at a friend's house sipping tea under the speckled shade of one of her spidery vine maples. We talked for some time about our very similar childhoods: the emotional trauma we had both experienced and how it had affected our adult lives. And though she too experienced moments of excruciating insecurity, she was thriving. It seemed everything she touched turned to gold.

"I don't understand how you do it," I said. "Nothing seems to work out for me."

"Monica, what are you talking about? Stop that."

"Well, I feel like I can't do anything. That I will never make my mark. I'm a mess. I'm not good enough."

Instead of patting me on the shoulder or giving me a hug and saying, "You can do anything you put your mind to," she simply took a sip of tea, looked me straight in the eyes, and said, "Then you won't."

"Won't what?" I questioned.

"Be good enough. You won't do anything." She shrugged.

Wow. That hit me hard. And you know what? She was right. I alone am responsible for my emotional well-being. It's up to me to do what I need to do to be the best me I can be. So if you are lost in that dark, dank pit of self-neglect, insecurity, shame, or emotional trauma, rise up, Witch, and heal thyself.

Out of Balance

For a lot us, maintaining that perfect outer persona comes at a high price. We live with having to continually push down suppressed feelings of guilt and/or shame, which can be highly detrimental to us on so many levels. When we are out of balance with our emotions, it not only affects how we feel on a day-to-day basis but also affects us physically and spiritually. It affects our interactions with family, friends, and coworkers, and worst of all, it affects how we see ourselves.

Insecurity can make it very convenient for our fragile egos to play the victim card. I hate to admit it, but I've been there. And let's be real—confessing our part in the story of our own failings isn't an easy thing to do. It is much easier to place the blame on our upbringing or our current circumstances. Someone once told me that there is no failure: we either win in life or we learn. I don't know about you, but I've learned a lot!

Dealing with strong feelings, painful memories, insecurity, and shame can be frightening, but once you make a conscious decision to unlock your emo-

Dealing with strong feelings, painful memories, insecurity, and shame can be frightening, but once you make a conscious decision to unlock your emotional jail cell and be an active participant in freeing yourself from your own emotional baggage, you are on your way to a life that is in balance—body, mind, and spirit.

tional jail cell and be an active participant in freeing yourself from your own emotional baggage, you are on your way to a life that is in balance—body, mind, and spirit.

To help you along the way, I have put together a few tips, tricks, spells, and charms that are not a cure but may help you on your journey to a fuller life.

Go Smudge Yourself

Smoke has been used for fumigation and clearing space, purification and blessing, and healing and preservation for thousands of years in cultures all over the world. The use of a smudge stick or bundle is actually a modern take on a collection of very old practices from various cultures and belief systems. You can use smudging to cleanse yourself of negative energies, past traumas, or bad experiences.

Smudge bundles can be found at any metaphysical store, but your rituals will be that much more meaningful if you make your own. Although almost any herb can be used to smudge, here are some common herbs whose sacred spirits vibrate a bit deeper than their physical constituents.

BAY

When added to your smudge bundle, these leaves add a big punch. Known for their protective, purifying, calming, and healing smoke, bay leaves are also a mood booster.

CEDAR

Cedar provides a wonderful purifying, protective, and sweet-smelling smoke that burns slowly, which makes it great for ritual use, especially for beginners.

EUCALYPTUS

Eucalyptus provides an energizing boost to your smudge bundle—great for healing and protection.

LAVENDER

The purifying, protective smoke of this fragrant herb also lends an air of peace and harmony to your smudge bundle.

Lemongrass

Lemongrass provides an energizing and refreshing smoke that also encourages clarity and focus.

Rosemary

The smoke of this Mediterranean herb encourages a sense of peace, purifies, and is excellent for removing negative vibrations.

Sage

Cleansing, healing and protective, the smoke of sage is the ultimate purifying herb. Note that due to its popularity, the sacred white sage (*Salvia apiana*) used to make the smudge bundles seen in any metaphysical store is now under threat. So when at all possible, use common garden sage (*Salvia officinalis*) in your bundles; it holds the same purifying power.

Sweetgrass

Sweetgrass produces a sweet-smelling smoke that is excellent for blessings or for attracting good spirits, but only after smudging with an herb that is meant to repel. (Never mix this herb with your smudge bundles meant for purification and cleansing—it defeats the purpose.)

Smudge Bundle

To make a smudge bundle, you will need:

- 4–10 sprigs of fresh herbs, 4–8 inches in length
- Twine (a natural fiber such as hemp or cotton)
- Scissors

Lay out your sprigs, making sure they are uniform and keeping the stems together.

Wrap some twine around the stems two to three times and knot it off. Wind the twine, working at an upward angle. Wrap it around the top of your bundle and continue the wrapping back down to the stem. Wrap it around twice and tie it off.

Dry your smudge by hanging the bundle in a paper bag or in a dark place for approximately two weeks.

Smudging Prayer to Clear Negative Energy

Light your smudge bundle and begin smudging at your crown. Repeat the following prayer as you move the smudge down your body:

> Cleanse my head so that I may remain clear and focused.
> Cleanse my eyes so that I may recognize true beauty in its many forms.
> Cleanse my heart so that I may express through the language of love.
> Cleanse my hands so that they may create for beauty and wonder.
> Cleanse my feet so that they might lead instead of follow.
> Cleanse my spirit so that I may soar.
> In the name of all that is flowing, wild, and free,
> Let the smoke cleanse away all negativity.
> Blessed be.

Sage Smudge Spray

For a little smudging on the go, try this nifty smudge spray. Keep it in your bag or at the office for those times when you really feel the need to promote healing vibrations. You will need:

- 2-ounce glass bottle with a spray head
- 1 ounce distilled water

- 1 teaspoon vodka/pure grain alcohol

- 10 drops sage essential oil

- 4 drops lavender essential oil

- Pinch of sea salt

Put the ingredients in the bottle and charge it to purify and promote healing vibrations. (I always use the energy of the full moon, but feel free to charge in your own way.)

Spell for Balance and Well-Being

This is a great early morning meditation that promotes a sense of balance and well-being and helps you maintain a harmonious vibe throughout the day. You will need an incense blend for this spell. Choose one of my recipes below or create your own special blend.

Get up early and find a nice, relaxing place outside to sit facing east. Say:

Spirits of the east, I welcome this new dawn.
Let your gentle touch dissolve all negativity.
Stress, strife, and anxiety, be gone.
In the name of air, wind, and peace,
Let the magic take hold.
So mote it be.

Light the incense. Sit in a comfortable position, allowing the breeze to clear away the negative residue that has built up from any emotional trauma, stress, or chaos in your life. Allow the smoke from the incense to draw in harmony and peace.

Incense Blend for Balance and Wisdom

2 parts sage (for wisdom)

1 part lavender (for balance)

1 part sandalwood (for inner strength)

½ part frankincense (for reflection and meditation)

Incense Blend for Well-Being

1 part cedarwood (for protection)

½ part lavender (for peace and balance)

½ part sandalwood (for healing)

The Choice Is Yours

Choosing to release your internal turmoil takes effort and intention. Smudging yourself once and calling it good isn't going to cut it. Waking every single day with the intention of choosing happiness and healing and following through with a solid plan is a good start. Remember, dear Witch, choose yourself over negativity, choose yourself over self-doubt, choose yourself over insecurity, and go live your dreams.

Monica Crosson (Concrete, WA) has been a practicing witch and educator for over thirty years and is a member of Evergreen Coven. She is the author of The Magickal Family and Wild Magical Soul and is a regular contributor to the Llewellyn annuals as well as magazines such as Enchanted Living and Witchology.

Illustrator: Bri Hermanson

Dealing with Real Darkness

Diana Rajchel

I hadn't stolen anyone's husband. No one experienced homelessness, unemployment, or jail because of me. Certainly, people don't like what I have to say at times. I am impatient with vanity, and more impatient when credit does not go where it is due. But my cumulative behavior for this lifetime leans more toward "hex her once and forget it" than "she must be destroyed."

Yet someone—and yes, I know exactly who—put a death curse on me.

In early 2015, life gave me quite a few slaps. Because of improbable occurrences, I found myself struggling with situational depression and an inability to move out of a negative cycle with my romantic partners. I felt bad, but I'd felt worse. I was looking for an end to the trouble. Then the thoughts came—the dark ones, the "call someone right now" thoughts. Often they came with specific images, the type that made the first season of *American Horror Story* look like a sweet little comedy.

Suicidal ideation is dangerous, tricky, and nasty—especially when your chemical makeup inclines you to it. Mine, however, did not. Suicidal ideation when you do not have the neurochemistry to match is scary as hell *because you know that the thoughts you're having aren't actually yours.*

Someone—and yes, I know exactly who—put a death curse on me....It took a gargantuan act of will to affirm to myself that I was experiencing something real. It took a second such act to reach out to a friend of mine, who has some gifts, for help.

It took a gargantuan act of will to affirm to myself that I was experiencing something real. It took a second such act to reach out to a friend of mine, who has some gifts, for help. I really had to fight off my own embarrassment and shame, this despite me being the one people usually reach out to when they find themselves in a similar situation. I have solid skills when it comes to keeping a tight house energetically—and yet I couldn't find a way to stop this.

This friend of mine listened to me, supported me, and believed me. With relatively little pulling of strings, we found both the person casting the curse and the being hired to torment me. By the end of our thirty-minute conversation, I found myself sitting very still as an ancient death deity inspected me, considered my side of the interaction, and

announced I had "too much potential to waste." Murdering me would deprive the world of something very interesting.

Having experienced a relationship with a sociopath who had said the same thing about me, this was perhaps not as reassuring as it could have been.

Over the next eighteen hours, I was given a vision of the spell needed to revoke all the magic used against me. I also received advice on how to make sure the energy never channeled to me again. It is not a well-known spell technique. It is also not the sort of thing that would be wise to share. Before this incident, I had never had visions. I have a flexible imagination and can pore over spell books and folklore and from there cobble together a series of symbols into a story-like whole. People have taken these symbol stories of mine and used them successfully for themselves.

This time, however, images of clearly assembled spell components flashed in my mind. There was no mining books for symbols. Here and there I heard questions: What modern invention could bring about this effect? What tools are available these days? I realized I was having a technology delivered straight to my deep mind, and this spirit was asking me to improve upon their art. This spirit was also doing its best to teach me how to break its power.

Another twenty-four hours later, I had performed the spell and walked free from that curse. The suicidal ideation stopped completely within a day, but the depression did not recede. I was still in a bad situation. Like most magick delivered by a competent hand, it leveraged what was already happening in my own life. I had reason to be depressed, and it increased my depression. I had reason to feel trapped and ungrounded, and the working took advantage of that, too. The most effective curses rely on the target to already feel blighted. I acknowledged these issues, wrote them down to discuss with my therapist, and attempted to walk off my emotions related to the situation.

But then I had to digest the fact that someone really had tried to kill me. And they had used magic—the thing that had always been my safe place—to do it.

Are you f____ kidding me? Why????

I already knew that *why* didn't matter. Over the course of my work at a domestic violence shelter, I had come to understand why abusers abuse. From there I had recognized the soul-disease in my own family and how it had shaped me.

I decided I wanted to reshape myself to be someone more capable of love and trust, but it's a difficult road even without metaphysical battles thrown in. Just stepping onto the path of changing myself had triggered a series of attacks. Changing yourself sends a signal to those who would control you that they are about to lose something.

Just stepping onto the path of changing myself had triggered a series of attacks. Changing yourself sends a signal to those who would control you that they are about to lose something.

I also knew that the person who had done this really knew nothing about me but imagined plenty. How others see you often has nothing to do with who you really are. It's important to keep that in mind when someone's toxicity boils over onto you. In someone's mind, I had failed to play the role they had assigned to me. When I didn't stick to that script, they had sought out tools to eliminate me. This is what narcissists and other poisonous people do. These types are in every community, and some of them know their way around a magic wand.

When we talk about darkness in the occult, we imply certain divisions: demons and shadow people over here, angels and fairies over there, gods and ancestors somewhere in the middle. But after you walk this path and start doing the work—as in fingernails buried in the dirt work—the divisions disappear. Everything—every being, every energy, every disease—is a neutral party. Whether something is good or bad depends on what you do with it. Magick is, now and forever, the double-edged blade, used to harm and to heal.

None of the spirits we seek out and honor are inherently evil. Real evil lies within the human breast alone; things we might label evil from these spirits are just impartial nature. Demons and other spirits don't summon themselves. Curses don't just happen. Ancestors, at some point, were and still are deeply *human*, and that's why the worst curses always hang out in the DNA. It's humans who have the stories, the dramas, and the wounds at the bottoms of their souls. Humans tell the stories and keep believing the stories they tell themselves. This goes on until something wakes them up and one person decides to change their story.

All evil and all good lie within the human psyche.

Even opportunistic exploitation from metaphysical parasites stems from diseases within our psychic systems. Whether the infected person turns that energy inward or outward depends entirely on the character they have cultivated within themselves. That all depends on the stories playing in the back of their mind.

In the era in which I write this, we are living in dark times—some argue that we live in the darkest timeline. Anyone anywhere can start their day minding their own business and end it in the middle of a violent tragedy. The conditions of the world have caused a lot of people to come unhinged, and the increased ease of access not just to magickal knowledge but to tools of explicit destruction have only increased the arsenal of those addicted to despair.

While I can send out a well-wish that no one who reads this suffers as I have, that isn't realistic. There are many situations that can open the gateway that causes someone to snap, such as illness, suicide, or the pressures of trying just to survive. There is no way to prepare for all possibilities. To attempt to do so becomes a disease in and of itself.

What I can do is point out some lesser-known tools and encourage everyone to take better care of their souls.

Some of this will sound too difficult, and perhaps right now it is for some of you. If you're in a situation where you're fighting something or someone off, just do what you can. Some days, survival is the only win you get. Accept that the tools of beginning witchcraft may not always work. There are energies in this world that sage and Florida water just can't fend off. When that happens, you must go within, and if you don't find weapons awaiting, you're going to have to create your own. To do so requires wit, grounding, and a commitment to seeking joy over despair.

Screen Your Physical and Mental Health on a Regular Basis

Often, if you are dealing with spiritual nastiness, good mental health support workers will remind you that you're not crazy. It also helps if they do not subscribe to the belief that magical thinking is a disease. Persistent searching can reveal those who accept magickal lifestyles.

A great deal of magickal attack relies on the inherent trauma of the target. Also, it can in and of itself be traumatizing. Getting continuous care can't always prevent the trauma, but it coaches you in the tools needed to combat the feelings of helplessness and fear.

Reach Out

For many who undergo metaphysical attacks, asking for help is the hardest part. It's embarrassing to admit that you're a target—or that someone is making successful hits on and in your life. You may need to pick and choose how and to whom you reach out. Certain corners of the Pagan community sometimes take a certain amount of glee in accusing people of fabrication or worse when they do reach out for help. I've had to help more than one person in trouble who really did try to get help and ended up with significant psychic injuries because of that behavior.

For many who undergo metaphysical attacks, asking for help is the hardest part. It's embarrassing to admit that you're a target—or that someone is making successful hits on and in your life.

Reach out anyway. There are experienced practitioners who have good discernment. The legitimately most helpful and powerful magick workers tend not to be the celebrities or the chest-beaters. They do what they do, they do it well, and when the spirit moves them to help, they do so.

Strangers Can Reduce Danger

As is the case in nearly all intimate violence, the worst attacks usually come from the people closest to you. If you can't figure out where the bad energy keeps coming from, reach out to a shaman or spirit worker with a good reputation. If you aren't sure where to look, visit your local occult shop. If something about your local occult shop makes you feel unsafe, then call a shop in a different town or even a different part of the country. California Bay Area metaphysical shops are especially rich with experienced spirit workers trained to help in tough situations. Yes, be prepared to pay the spiritual people. The work they do is genuinely dangerous, often requires complex training, and often comes with physical after-effects. Plus, they have to take the time to explain everything to you and possibly show you how to keep whatever is happening from happening again.

Expand Your Toolbox

When people know what you're going to use to erase their negativity, some find ways to ensure that those go-tos fail. This is one reason people include sage and palo santo in cursing work. You may need to venture outside your culture of origin—or dive deeper into it—to find new cleansing and protection tools. The following short list includes a few less common but potent tools for eradicating harassing spells, spirits, and energies. Use these tools sparingly—while not true of all, some are still made from dwindling natural resources. Also, when you overuse any substance, what you use it on can develop an immunity. Make sure you switch out your tools of choice from time to time.

Tibetan Spirit-Purging Incense

This incense is indeed made by Tibetan Buddhist monks, prayed over 108 times and mixed by hand. When burned, it drives out the most stubborn of spirits. All you need to do is sprinkle a small amount on a hot incense charcoal, open a window, and wave goodbye. One limitation: it only works on actual spirits. Hostile faeries, astral projections, and servitors are immune. It also can't clear out spell energy.

Baker's Ammonia

Conjure workers often use ammonia as a spiritual cleansing agent in their homes. Ammonia strips off everything, good or bad. Baker's ammonia is a powdered version of this chemical and is used for making flatbreads. A little bit of this powder where you sense destructive energy erases it. It works particularly well on sigils, spells, and poppets. Just be careful to avoid erasing anything with energies you want to keep.

Black Salt

This does not refer to Hawaiian black salt, which has different protective qualities. Traditional black salt comes from mixing the scrapings in a seasoned cast iron skillet with regular iodized salt. The iron increases the protection level of the salt significantly. Sprinkle this on your windowsills, in the corners of your home, and around your baseboards. You can find recipes for black salt online, or you can purchase it from any reputable occult supplier.

Aegirine

Crystals get overused and worn out, so choose them sparingly. Aegirine works like souped-up tourmaline. Like tourmaline, aegirine absorbs negative energy. But it goes a step further: this black stone can absorb entire spirit attachments. If you catch a parasite while doing a working, aegirine can absorb it completely. Like tourmaline, the stone can get full, so make sure to place it in the sunshine to burn off its old absorptions before wearing or carrying it again.

Switch It Up

If you normally use candle magick, switch to spraying potions. Or if you normally only do energy work, deliberately cast a spell using physical tools. The more varied your methods, the more you can counter and minimize what's coming at you.

Education over Fear

Learn about what's happening to you from as many sources as you can. Start with divination—see if you or someone not connected to the situation can get a clear view of your situation. Learn all you can about the techniques used, the spirits summoned, and, if possible, the desired effects of the work. If you truly educate yourself about things you perceive as evil, you can shift the dynamic. You may find you need to do some ancestor work, or you may discover that the negative patch is the result of forgetting to keep a promise to a spirit. If you can maintain an attitude of curiosity throughout the ordeal, you will get through it that much faster.

. . . .

The energy of malediction and malevolence is complicated and deeply intertwined with our daily lives. It also exploits our human tendency to withdraw when we are hurting the most—and thus need the most help. When these dark things happen, keep reaching out, even if doing so uses up all the energy you have. Help will find you, no matter how deep into the storm you may be.

Diana Rajchel *is a witch, spirit worker, and psychic reader in San Francisco, CA. She is the author of* Urban Magick: A Guide for the City Witch, *among other titles. She specializes in helping people in touchy metaphysical situations. You can reach out to her at dianarajchel.com.*

Illustrator: Rik Olson

Witchy Living

DAY-BY-DAY WITCHCRAFT

Magical Morning Practices: Making the Most of These Everyday Liminal Moments

Astrea Taylor

Mornings are like portals. We emerge from a deep, dream-filled trance state and traverse a huge mental realm to shift our mindset to be more productive and alert. That's no small feat! Mornings are everyday magical, liminal moments. However, not everyone treats them as a special time.

Years ago, before I developed my own magical morning practices, I would leap out of bed and rush through my morning tasks as quickly as possible. I was definitely not a morning person, and I gave little thought to the transition between sleep and waking. My only focus was making it to work on time.

When a friend confided to me that they purposefully woke up early in order to "take in the day," it was unfathomable to me. Waking up any earlier than I already did was simply unthinkable. However, when I actually tried it, my worldview changed drastically.

Through my magical morning practices, I started to become more present and grounded in my body. I took time to connect with my intuition and spirit. Now, with this added focus, I

Through my magical morning practices, I started to become more present and grounded in my body. I took time to connect with my intuition and spirit. Now, with this added focus, I often retain a magical mindset for the entire day.

often retain a magical mindset for the entire day. Sometimes I can even transcend some of the mundane drama as well. At first, waking up an extra fifteen minutes early was a burden, but now I've found that I don't miss the sleep. The added pleasures of creating a witchy morning practice greatly make up for it.

This article explores a few of my favorite ways to make your day more magical. I do some of these activities every day, such as the magical morning beverage. Others are included only if my intuition guides me to do them, such as calling upon a spirit. It's nearly impossible to perform all of these practices every day unless you have a few hours, but you'll probably be able to fit in more of them than you think. Explore the ones you're guided to—use your intuition and do whatever you feel will aid you each morning.

Write Down Your Dreams

There's nothing witchier than connecting to the unconscious. Dreams are the canvases upon which our unconscious mind paints. We're intensely connected to those stories that play out in our mind. We create every place and person, and they're all meaningful representations of how we feel. Dream journaling connects us to our deep trance state and shows us where we put our energy.

Keep a writing utensil and a dream journal by your bed. As soon as you wake up, write down everything that you can remember. Ponder the meanings of your dreams later in the day, when you're in a different mindset. You may also ask a trusted friend about them for more insight.

Move Your Body Intuitively

Every morning after I get out of bed, my body expresses the need to roll out the stiff muscles. I move intuitively—extending an arm here, stretching a hamstring there. I release the stiffness and compression, making space for new energy to bloom in my body.

You might think that moving your body isn't a witchy practice, but it most certainly is. Whenever we move, we release stagnant energy from our body. We wake up our muscles and charge them with the ability to do the work we need to accomplish that day.

If music helps you find those intuitive movements, use it. It's a mood booster, and can either extend your liminal state of mind further or wake you up more, if that's what you wish. Moving is a great activity to do while your coffee or tea is brewing.

Magical Morning Beverage

Whether you drink coffee, tea, or some other morning beverage, you can easily elevate your process to make it more magical. To do so, take your time as you make it, being aware of every movement. Connect

with the elements—warm your hands by the heat or the fire, feel the energy of the water or ice, relish the aromas, and savor the earthiness of the tea or coffee.

If you're not fully awake at this point, that's okay too. You don't have to be completely present to make a morning beverage magical. You can retain your liminal state as you make it. There's nothing wrong with keeping a soft mind at this time. You'll wake up soon enough!

Once your beverage is made, take a moment to appreciate it. Feel the spirit of the beverage and align with it. Wrap your hands around the glass or mug and inhale. Recite a spell or an intention to make your beverage truly magical, if you wish. One of my favorites is this: *This drink awakens the magic within me.*

Sometimes I stir my coffee clockwise three times or add a sprinkle of cinnamon for good luck. I've also been known to pour some into an espresso cup for deity or dribble a bit onto the ground for nature spirits.

Sit at Your Altar

I love my morning altar. It's where I really wake up. It doubles as my center altar for magical practices, and has tarot cards, a candle, a lighter, some burnable herbs, my book of shadows, a pen, a few stones, some magic tools, a Tibetan singing bowl, and a coaster for my beverage. It's situated next to a small sofa that overlooks an eastern-facing window, where the sun rises. As I sip my coffee, I align with the energy of the altar and all the magic stored there.

Morning Divination

One of my favorite things to do in the morning is to draw tarot cards or runes. I pull one for my energy, one for the external energy at hand, one for advice from the gods or spirits, and more for whatever else I wish to know about. Divination often gives me more information about the day and helps me mentally prepare for it. This helps me take a moment to center my energy and meditate so I can be more in charge and less reckless with my responses.

Meditate or Feel the Day

Sometimes when I'm sitting before my morning altar, something tells me to be still. With closed eyes and deep breaths, I ground into my body and still my mind. In the present moment, I can feel both the energy I'm radiating and the energy of the day. I notice where I'm holding tension and listen to what my intuition tells me about it. I align my chakras and adjust my energy, healing myself.

Set an Intention

Declaring your will for the day is an empowering act. It gives you a certain focus, one you can come back to at various times throughout the day. Use "I" statements in your intentions to give yourself the power to accomplish them. If you like, you can write your intentions in your book of shadows. You can even perform additional divination to get more information about how your intention will fare throughout the day.

Call Upon a Spirit or Deity

When I need extra assistance or if I'm longing for something more, there's nothing like lighting a candle and calling upon *big energy* in my morning practice. I've called upon gods and spirits, including my deceased loved ones and spirit guides. When I do this, I light the candle and speak their name out loud. I listen for their soft voice in my head. I sometimes have an offering for them, but usually I just sit with them and send them energy and receive energy from them. Sometimes I let them choose a tarot card or rune as a way to communicate with me.

Shower Power

Everyone knows that showers and baths are wonderful ways to wake up and get clean, but they can also be magical. Every morning, as I wash my body, I imagine that I'm washing both my physical body and my energetic body. Sometimes I open my chakras and release any stagnant energy. I imagine that the undesired energy flows away from me and goes down the bathtub drain. If I need extra energetic cleansing, a handful of Epsom salt gently smoothed into my skin usually works.

After cleansing, I like to infuse myself with a certain kind of energy. Sometimes I imagine that the water is a beautiful color that seeps into my skin, recharging me completely. Other times I use soaps or body washes that are made with essential oils. I associate the different aromas with different qualities, and use whichever one I want. For example, if I want spiritual centering, I use a lavender soap. If I need a sweet, gentle day, I use a tangerine-vanilla soap. These aromas ground me into my preferred energy and enrich my morning experience. I often buy several different kinds of soap so I can use whichever one suits my needs that morning.

Other times I use soaps or body washes that are made with essential oils. I associate the different aromas with different qualities... If I want spiritual centering, I use a lavender soap. If I need a sweet, gentle day, I use a tangerine-vanilla soap.

Dress Yourself Enchantingly

Whenever we choose our clothing and jewelry for the day, we're performing a magical practice. Choose the colors, fabrics, and silhouette based on your intention for the day and what you need to help manifest your goals.

Some mornings, if I know I'm going to be out of my depth, I'll enchant my clothing. For example, if I'm going to a big city or a big meeting, I'll envision protective armor over my cardigan, or I'll wear a piece of jewelry that has been enchanted to give me strength. It only takes a moment to charm or enchant an object. To do so, hold it and focus on your intention as you push your energy into it. If you wish, you can recite your intention as well, such as this one: *Strength of mind is truly mine.*

Consider hiding something on your person that will give you extra energy if you need it. It could be a charm, a bag of herbs tied around your waist, a small stone in your pocket, or a long necklace tucked into your shirt. You can also draw a sigil on yourself using an essential oil diluted in carrier oil. This last practice is extremely beneficial if you need to keep your accessories light, such as while traveling through an airport.

Check In with the Magical Community

I check in with the people in my home by petting my cats and kissing my partner. It's important to share the love with them. If I have time, I'll go online and check in with the magical community. I keep it spiritual by limiting my exposure to supportive people only. I'll likely get into the news and drama later that day, but for that moment, it's nice to see only friendly faces.

If you chafe at the thought of social media in the morning, you might consider visiting a pagan-only site. Another good place to visit is an astrological site, where you can read your horoscope to learn more about the energy of the day.

Greet the Sun

Whether I'm gazing at the sun through the window or standing outside beneath it, I adore saying hello to the sun, our solar system's beautiful, bright star. Feeling the sun's starlight wash over my face is a magical experience. Every dawn is a new day, and the sun is a powerhouse of energy. Align your energy with it to feel the momentous energy of the day and to feel empowered. Appreciate its shine, light, heat, and energy.

Take a Moment

After I leave my house, I stand outside and look around at my yard. I breathe in the fresh air and notice the weather, the quality of the sunshine, the temperature, and the wind. I take it all in and sometimes talk with the animals outside as well. Weather permitting, I visit my little garden to appreciate its growth and greenery.

Consciously Shift into the Day

After my magical morning practices are over, I like to consciously shift into my productive mindset. With a deep breath, I decide to start my day and make the magic happen. This practice takes only a moment, but it really helps me transition from my magical morning practice into a more worldly mindset.

. . . .

Good morning! The best thing about these magical morning practices is that they set an energetic tone that can carry you through the entire day. Of course, this isn't a complete list of magical morning practices. If you think of other activities that would aid you in beginning the day with a positive attitude and a clear intention, feel free to add them to your repertoire.

Astrea Taylor *is the author of* Intuitive Witchcraft: How to Use Intuition to Elevate Your Craft (*Llewellyn, 2020*) *and the forthcoming* Air Magic (*Llewellyn, 2021*). *Astrea blogs as* Starlight Witch *for Patheos Pagan and teaches workshops and rituals at various pagan gatherings across the country. She currently lives in Southwest Ohio, where she co-leads the fire dancing group Aurora Fire.*

Illustrator: M. Kathryn Thompson

Dining with the Goddess

James Kambos

My grandfather would always reach down and scoop up a handful of rich Ohio soil before planting his crops. He'd pause to inhale its earthy scent before crumbling it through his fingers. Then for a brief moment he'd close his eyes as if praying. Maybe he was. In his way he was thanking Mother Earth, maybe the Goddess herself, for the life-giving soil in which he was about to plant his seeds.

The memory of this ritual has stayed with me.

On our Ohio farm, we raised corn, wheat, and soybeans. From the orchard we were blessed with apples and cherries. Grapes and raspberries grew abundantly. We also raised cattle, sheep, hogs, and chickens.

It's easy to understand why, after being raised close to the land, I developed a deep respect for the earth's blessings. Early on I saw food as a gift from the Goddess.

Today, as I think about our farm's bounty and the deep reverence my grandfather showed the soil, I am inspired to treat any mealtime as a mini ritual of thanks to the Goddess. As I shop for groceries, prepare a meal, and set the table, I feel as if I am truly dining with the Goddess. I treat the entire process of food shopping, meal prep, and eating as a time to be mindful of and thankful to the Goddess who has blessed me with the food that sustains me.

> **I am inspired to treat any mealtime as a mini ritual of thanks to the Goddess. As I shop for groceries, prepare a meal, and set the table, I feel as if I am truly dining with the Goddess.**

In our busy digital, Instagram world, it's easy to rush through mealtime, and the steps leading up to it, without giving a thought to what a blessing our food really is. Our meals needn't be elaborate, but they should be meaningful.

As Pagans and Witches, most of us follow a nature-based calendar of the year. Some of the sabbats are centered around food and harvests. But why wait to give thanks only a few times a year for the food the Goddess has blessed us with? Turn mealtime, even setting the table, into a mini ritual of thanks. Learn to look at your dining room table or kitchen counter as more than just a place to eat. Begin to see them as a type of altar—a place to commune with the divine.

Whether you're eating with family or alone, take time every day to dine with the Goddess. Taking the time to truly savor the food will help to create a magical moment. Selecting, preparing, and serving the food will take on a pleasant new meaning.

Here are some tips to make your total food experience a magical one and an opportunity to show your gratitude to the Goddess.

Behold the Bounty of the Goddess

The bounty of the Goddess is all around us. We just need to truly see it and appreciate it as we shop for food. Beholding the bounty she provides us with is the first step in dining with the Goddess. This is what you should experience when you go grocery shopping. Don't just rush through the supermarket shoving food into your cart haphazardly. Take your time. Look at what you're buying. After all, this is what's going to fuel you and your family as you work and play.

First, look at the colors: the yellow squash, red tomatoes, and orange peppers. Aren't they beautiful? But don't stop there. Lemons, oranges, and grapefruit—these are associated with the sun and energy.

The greens come in every shade, from dark green kale and broccoli to pale green Granny Smith apples.

What about berries? Blueberries and raspberries aren't just pretty; they're also great for your eyes. And who can resist blackberries or strawberries?

As you shop, don't forget to admire all the textures too. The knobby feel of a potato and the glossy smoothness of an eggplant are also gifts from the Goddess.

There are many other fruits, vegetables, and legumes to admire, but you get my point. Really take the time to admire these sacred gifts from the Goddess. It'll enhance your entire food experience.

Also, when shopping for fruits and vegetables, don't forget to stop at your local farmers' market. It's a good way to get to know the people who work directly with Mother Earth to bring us our food.

If you eat poultry, meat, or fish, as you select a cut, please say a silent prayer of thanks to the animal's spirit. It gave its life to help sustain yours.

In the Kitchen with the Goddess

If there's one room in the home most closely associated with the Goddess, it's the kitchen. It's the temple of the Goddess. It's here that we store and cook our food. It's here that food is usually eaten. Even in a modern home, it's associated with the hearth. The kitchen is the hub of the home. It's also where many non-food activities take place. The kids' homework or craft projects may be done here.

In short, the kitchen is a sacred space, a temple, to the Goddess. Treat it that way when you cook and eat. A peaceful vibration will fill your entire home if you do this.

Let's talk about the sacred act of cooking. The Goddess will love and favor you if you treat cooking as a magical act instead of a chore. Think about it. Cooking is magical. When you cook, you're taking part in a transformation, just like magic. When you peel, dice, slice, or sauté any fruit or vegetable, you're transforming the original food into something new and wonderful.

The kitchen is a sacred space, a temple, to the Goddess. Treat it that way when you cook and eat. A peaceful vibration will fill your entire home if you do this.

When you cook with the Goddess in mind and are fully aware, you'll notice you're working with the elements. For example, fruits, vegetables, grains, and most meats symbolize the earth element. Preparing soups or broth represents water. The heat source you use for cooking brings in the fire element. Air is represented by the aromas you create.

Let's not forget how magical the kitchen utensils can be. Many basic kitchen items are clearly linked to the Goddess or magic in general. A pot or bowl represents the cauldron and the Goddess. Also, in a pot or bowl is where a magical transformation will take place. Any kitchen knife definitely symbolizes the magical athame. Even the simple act of stirring is magical. It resembles a cauldron being stirred.

When you're in the kitchen, you're definitely in a sacred space. The food you prepare there needn't be fancy, but it should be prepared with magical intent.

Your Table, Your Altar

The kitchen is a sacred space, and the act of cooking is a magical way to connect with the Goddess. It only makes sense that if you wish to dine with the Goddess, the place where you eat should also be a sacred space. To make your mealtime truly sacred, think of the physical place in which you eat as an altar. If I'm eating at my kitchen counter or at my dining room table, I think of that space as an altar.

Mealtime is a special, sacred time. I view it as a mini ritual. You may eat in a cozy kitchen nook, at a kitchen island, or in an elegant dining room. But what is really important is that you eat with a magical attitude. This is a time to commune with the Goddess. For this reason, please try to avoid gulping down your food while standing over the kitchen sink or while driving.

Since your eating space/table should be treated like an altar, set it like one. Do use a tablecloth or placemats, and napkins as well. Nice paper ones are fine. Dishes don't need to be fancy, but try not to use chipped or cracked ones. A small vase of flowers or a bowl of fruit is a nice touch. As with any altar, try to have it set with at least one candle. The act of lighting a candle can draw positive vibrations. These are a few ideas. Setting your table with seasonal décor also creates a pleasant dining experience.

To enhance the idea that this is a ritual, wash your hands before eating. As you sit, thank the Goddess by saying (or thinking) a prayer for the bounty you are about to receive. Saying a simple "thank you" will do.

As you eat, do so mindfully. Think of where the food comes from. Savor the colors and textures. With each bite, think of how the food is improving your general well-being.

These are things you can do even when eating alone. This way of eating—dining with the Goddess in mind—will bring magic into your daily life.

· · · · · · · · · · · ·

The concept of connecting with Mother Earth and mother goddess figures to give thanks for food and eating is not new. Nameless, faceless agricultural goddess figures have been venerated by the human race for thousands of years. Today, when you pay tribute to the Goddess or to a specific deity as you eat, you're taking part in a human ritual that dates back to the days before recorded history.

James Kambos *writes about folk magic, spells, and herbalism. His interest in folk magic began by watching his mother and grandmother prepare spells from their native Greece. He writes and paints from his home in the beautiful hills of southern Ohio.*

Illustrator: Bri Hermanson

Magical Habit Building

Melissa Tipton

Why does positive change come so easy to a lucky few, while the rest of us claw our way uphill, only to find ourselves too often sliding right back to where we started? For years, I thought my own pesky habits boiled down to mere laziness. When I did manage to implement a healthy routine, it was a welcome but mysterious victory. Then I discovered the work of Charles Duhigg. In his 2012 book *The Power of Habit*, he outlines a no-guesswork sequence for crafting intentional habits, and I was instantly intrigued. Could I blend this with my magical practice to produce powerful results? As I discovered, the answer was a resounding *yes*. It is well within your reach to transform your own life as well. Let's look at how to use your magical practice to forge the habits you want and ditch the ones you don't.

Anatomy of a Habit

To change a habit, we first need to break down what, exactly, a habit is. There are three components to a habit. The first is a cue. This is what triggers the habit and starts you down the predictable path, be it polishing off that last cookie or skipping meditation. The second component is a routine. Once the cue is registered, the routine kicks in, whether that's rummaging around in the cupboard or getting lost in a Netflix hole instead of pulling out the meditation cushion. The third component is the reward. You wouldn't be engaged in this routine if your brain didn't attach it to a reward, and a sequence of actions becomes a habit once the brain starts to crave and expect this reward.

While research shows that we can't eradicate a habit, we *can absolutely* change the routine—

> **While…we can't eradicate a habit, we can *absolutely* change the routine…Let's say you regularly end up on the couch watching TV every night instead of tending to your goal of meditating…With exploration and some magical tools, you can unlock what the accompanying cue and reward are…and then use that information to change your routine.**

and this is huge. Let's say you regularly end up on the couch watching TV every night instead of tending to your goal of meditating or journaling with your tarot cards. With exploration and some magical tools, you can unlock what the accompanying cue and reward are (and the reward might be surprisingly different from what you think) and then use that information to change your routine of loafing on the couch.

What's in It for Me?

A routine doesn't stick unless our brain starts to anticipate and crave the associated reward, so an important key to unlocking a habit is to identify the reward. Start by brainstorming the possibilities in your journal. When you plop down on the couch and turn on the tube, are you getting any of the following:

- A feeling of peace and calm after a stressful day

- A distraction from something you've been worrying about

- Enjoyable time snuggling up next to your partner

- The feeling of being engaged and interested in an activity

- Something else

This inquiry requires some experimentation to make sure you're really hitting on the actual reward motivating your habit. To aid in this process, here's a simple yet effective ritual.

Ritual of Rewards

All you'll need for this ritual is a candle, a journal, and a writing utensil. I like to perform the ritual at night, so there's more contrast between dark and light when I ignite the candle, but it can be performed effectively at any time.

To prepare, copy the following passage into your journal so you can read it during the ritual.

I, [your name], ask for the guidance of [your preferred higher power(s)] in identifying the reward I am seeking when I engage in [describe the routine]. I ask that this information come to me in a way I can clearly and easily understand. Thank you.

With the candle unlit, sit comfortably and close your eyes. Bring your focus to your breath, and gently start to lengthen your inhales and exhales. Do this for at least a few rounds to bring yourself into a more calm and centered place. Then open your eyes and read aloud the passage you copied into your journal.

Prepare to light the candle as you say aloud:

This candle sheds light on parts unseen, bringing my awareness to what is most important for me to know right now.

Light the candle and gaze softly into the flame. Without trying to force any realizations or connections, simply allow yourself to stay curious. If you tend to get impatient, you might set a timer for ten to fifteen minutes, putting your mind at ease that you won't be there forever. Watch the flame for a few rounds of breath, then close your eyes. If any insights arise, open your eyes and jot them down in your journal before returning to eyes closed.

Don't worry if you don't feel like you've got everything figured out by the end of the ritual. This is meant to plant a seed that will continue to grow over the following week's guided practice. When you feel ready, end the ritual with thanks to any powers you called upon, and let the candle burn down on its own, if it's possible to do so safely.

Getting to the Root of the Habit

For the next five days, you're going to run some little experiments to help you see more clearly what, exactly, you're getting from your habit. Look back over your brainstorming notes, and come up with alternative ways to experience the possible desired outcomes you listed. These are the variables you'll be testing throughout the week to see which, if any, is the underlying reward that your brain craves.

For example, other ways to feel peace and calm after a long day might be taking a bubble bath, giving yourself a little scalp massage, or doing a ten-minute yin yoga routine. This isn't about trying to implement any of these options as a new habit—not yet. This is simply an experiment to see if something else scratches the underlying itch, thereby giving you insight into what the itch actually is.

If, for example, giving yourself a scalp massage satisfies the urge and you no longer feel like zoning out in front of the television, then it's reasonable to assume that what you were after was indeed feeling relaxed. If you think that perhaps you're motivated by having snuggle time with your partner, then cuddle up *without* the TV on and see if that satisfies the craving. Again, if it does, then you've identified the underlying reward connected to the routine. Now you have a new routine that you can substitute for the previous habit of sitting down and turning on the television.

Cue It Up

The next step is identifying the cue that triggers the habit. This might be a certain time of day, being around certain people, being in a particular place, a specific emotion, or a certain action that precedes the urge. Some examples of each include hitting a wall every afternoon around 2:00 and reaching for a sugary soda (time), hanging out with some old drinking buddies (people), being in a movie theater with the all-pervasive buttery popcorn aroma (place), feeling lonely or stressed (emotions), or logging in to Facebook (preceding action).

Perform the Ritual of Rewards again, this time using the following passage:

> I, [your name], ask for the guidance of [your preferred higher power(s)] in identifying the cue triggering [describe the routine]. I ask that this information come to me in a way that I can clearly and easily understand. Thank you.

Then, for the next five days, journal whenever the craving strikes and make a note of *each of the following*: the time of the craving, whom you're with, where you are, what you're feeling, and what you did just prior to experiencing the craving. At the end of five days, look over your notes for patterns. Maybe you find that the urge to get a sugary iced coffee arises only when you've been sitting at your desk for hours and you need a break. Great! This is valuable information, and now you can start experimenting with a new habit.

Putting It All Together

Now that you know your cue and your reward, it's time to start changing the routine. Using the above iced coffee example, when the cue strikes, make a plan to follow a new routine, such as giving yourself permission to go for a ten-minute walk and get some fresh air, go to the break room to chat with coworkers, play ten minutes of your favorite game app, or get an unsweetened iced tea instead. Choose *one* of these options beforehand so you're not deciding in the moment. The key is to make a plan ahead of time, well before the craving strikes, so you're not trying to figure anything out in crave-mode. Once you have your plan, write it down in your journal.

Get Your Witch On

To supercharge your efforts, bring in your magickal practice. Here are some great ways to help you stick to your new habit.

CREATE A REMINDER CRYSTAL

Choose a crystal using your intuition, or do a quick internet search for crystals related to your habit (for example, pyrite for money-related issues or sunstone for boosting confidence in your power to change). Cleanse the crystal by placing it in a bowl of salt overnight (discard the salt afterward) or by holding it in your hands and envisioning the crystal filling with pure, bright light, cleansing it of any and all harmful energies. Then charge the crystal with your new intention. While holding the crystal in your hands, repeat the following statement three times, ending with "And so it is."

> I *call upon this* [name of crystal] *to aid me in* [state your new routine]. [Repeat this statement three times.] And *so it is.*

Here is an example:

> I *call upon this hematite to aid me in taking a walk whenever I have a craving to smoke. I call upon this hematite to aid me in taking a walk whenever I have a craving to smoke. I call upon this hematite to aid me in taking a walk whenever I have a craving to smoke. And so it is.*

Then carry your reminder crystal with you, wear it as jewelry, or display it prominently, especially in the area where or during the time when you are most likely to be triggered.

CAST A WILLPOWER SPELL

On any given day, we have a finite amount of willpower, so having a plan for the times when our willpower is being challenged is a game changer. Over time, these plans become positive habits, so we no longer have to use our willpower reserves in those moments. The habit simply kicks in and off we go.

First off, identify hot-button situations where you're most likely to resort to the old habit. Examples include arguing with your kids, having to work late, being stuck in traffic, and so forth. If nothing comes to mind, you can use the same process you used for identifying cues. Let's say you notice that it's incredibly hard for you to resist getting an iced coffee when your coworker comes over to your desk and wants to gossip about everyone.

Having a plan for the times when our willpower is being challenged is a game changer. Over time, these plans become positive habits, so we no longer have to use our willpower reserves in those moments. The habit simply kicks in and off we go.

You realize that you feel uncomfortable and trapped in his cloud of toxic energy. Awesome! Now you can plan for this scenario.

Second, brainstorm other options for dealing with this trigger. You could kindly yet firmly let your coworker know you need to stay focused on a project and return to your work. You could excuse yourself and go to the restroom. You could be direct and explain to your coworker, without chastising or blaming him, that you enjoy his company (if that's actually the case) but don't want to use that time for gossip and would rather hear how his day is going, discuss that interesting new project you're both working on, etc. Write these options in your journal, then use the Ritual of Rewards format to get clarity on which option you're going to implement.

Third, practice the chosen option ahead of time. Visualize the scenario in your mind multiple times, with you carrying out the new behavior. Role-play it with a partner, even if it feels a little silly. Trust that this is building powerful energetic pathways that will make things much easier when you're in the hot seat.

Finally, cast a spell. I like to use this basic petition spell format:

I, [your name], ask for the guidance and aid of [your preferred higher power(s)] in [briefly describe the new action] when [briefly describe the hot-button scenario]. I ask that this unfold in accordance with the highest good, harming none. Thank you. So mote it be!

For example:

I, Karen Whittacre, ask for the guidance and aid of Athena and Apollo in kindly and firmly expressing that I need to focus on work when Tom wants to gossip. I ask that this unfold in accordance with the highest good, harming none. Thank you. So mote it be!

To cast your spell, create a sacred circle in whatever way you choose, and raise energy while visualizing yourself carrying out the new plan of action. You could use drumming, rattling, or hand clapping; visualization; movement; or any method you like. Do this until it feels like the energy has reached its peak and is about to "pop." Then read your petition spell three times, releasing the energy, perhaps by flinging your hands into the air. Give thanks and feel the excitement of choosing a new course of action when the situation arises.

Melissa Tipton *is a Structural Integrator, Reiki Master, and tarot reader who helps people live their most magical life through her healing practice,* Life Alchemy Massage Therapy. *She's the author of* Living Reiki: Heal Yourself & Transform Your Life *and* Llewellyn's Complete Book of Reiki. *Take online classes and learn more at getmomassage.com and yogiwitch.com.*

Illustrator: Tim Foley

Anchored Shields: Create an Energetic Safe Haven

Emily Carlin

We've all been in situations where external energies have negatively impacted our well-being. You can probably think of at least one area of your life where you're dealing with such a situation right now. Maybe you've got a negative worker or roommate; maybe it's a predatory romantic partner or a toxic relative that you can't quite cut out of your life; or maybe the area where you live is filled with negative emotions and stress.

As a practitioner of magick, you've probably tried to energetically shield yourself in these situations, with varying degrees of success. Shielding is one of the most critical skills for practitioners of all stripes. It keeps our energies safe from negative energy, whether it be ambient, unintentionally sent, or deliberately targeted. For short-term situations, like having a brief visit with a negative relative or walking through a room with people arguing, we can usually hold strong shields without issue. However, over time it can become quite draining, exhausting us and making our shields less effective. For long-term situations, such as a bad roommate, a toxic workplace, or protection on long-term housing, a better alternative is to use anchored shields.

For those who aren't familiar with it, shielding is the practice of forming a layer of protective energy around something, usually a person or place, in order to strengthen the barrier between it and the outside world and protect it from negative energy. The first shield most practitioners learn to create is the bubble shield. To cast a bubble shield, simply imagine a solid bubble of energy forming all the way around the person or place being shielded, like a soap bubble expanding around and encompassing them. This energetic bubble creates a barrier that negative energy can't pass through. If you've ever seen any of the Star Trek movies or television shows, think of what it looks like when they raise the ship's shields. You are seeing the characters essentially raise a bubble shield around their ship. This simple shield will protect you as long as you hold it in your mind. When you stop holding the shield in your mind, it will fade away. As you might imagine, it takes a fair amount of energy to maintain such a shield, particularly if it is under constant stress from incoming negative energy.

What Are Anchored Shields?

Anchored shields function in the same way as traditional shields in terms of how they protect against negative energies. Where they differ is in how they are fueled. Traditional shields, like the bubble shield just described, are powered entirely by the energy of the practitioner casting them. Anchored shields are sustained by an energy source external to the practitioner, usually some form of energetic battery created by the practitioner. This means the shield can be held for as long as the anchor has charge without any drain on the practitioner's personal reserves. Most anchors can be charged many times, meaning the shields they sustain can last indefinitely so long as they are maintained. This makes them far superior to traditional shields for any situation requiring warding for more than a few hours. Anchored shields are particularly well suited for long-term protection of people and places.

> **Anchored shields are sustained by an energy source external to the practitioner, usually some form of energetic battery created by the practitioner. This means the shield can be held for as long as the anchor has charge without any drain on the practitioner's personal reserves.**

The main drawback of an anchored shield is that it distances the practitioner from the situation at hand. When a practitioner actively maintains a shield, they become acutely aware of energetic nuances as they occur. Each jolt of negative energy that hits the shield is felt by the one holding it, allowing the source and severity of that negativity to be read. Tiring as it may be, holding an active shield can tell a practitioner a lot about a situation and thus can be a useful diagnostic tool. Anchored shields don't give the same level of energetic feedback because the practitioner becomes fully separate from the shield as soon as it is anchored. In practice this is really only a problem when a situation takes an unexpected turn for the worse. For example, if your bedroom is protected by an anchored shield that's ready

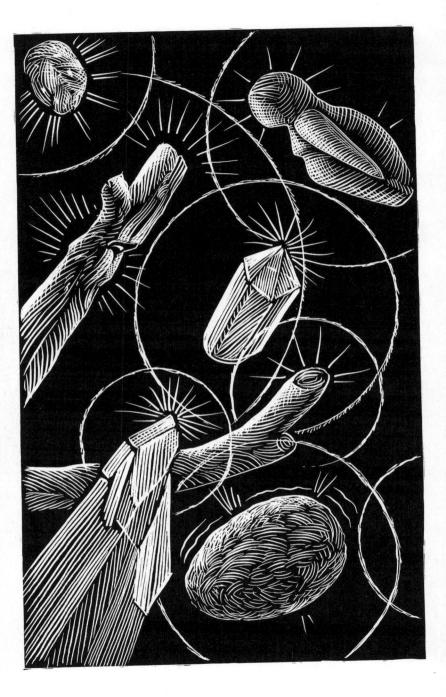

for a recharge and your roommates have a terrible row, the negative energy from the fight might completely drain your shield overnight and you could wake up to the unpleasant effects of stewing in negative energy all night. Of course, making sure the anchor is fully charged each day can circumvent this for all but the most unlikely of events. While not a perfect method, the benefits of anchored shielding for long-term protection outweigh any drawbacks.

Choosing an Anchor

Almost any physical object can be used to anchor a shield, but certain things are better suited than others for the job. The object serving as an anchor will function as both an energetic battery and a physical focus for the casting and recharging of the shield. This means that the object chosen should (1) have the physical capacity to store large amounts of energy, (2) energetically resonate with the purpose of the shield, and (3) resonate with the person or place being shielded.

The best anchors should have the physical capacity to hold enough energy to maintain a shield for a full month. All physical objects can hold power, but those made of stone, crystal, or wood tend to have the most intrinsic capacity. Stones and crystals are widely lauded for their ability to store energy, particularly granite, mica, quartz, and labradorite. Crystals generally have the best ability to hold energy, so they are favored for this purpose. Everyday rocks can serve as shield anchors as well, but the most effective ones will be those flecked with as much crystal as possible. Most crystals the size of a quarter or larger can hold enough energy for a decent shield, while the average rock should be a bit larger (ranging from golf ball size to full flagstones, depending on the composition and how often it will be recharged). Crystals are ideal for personal shields or those that need to be mobile, as their small size makes them easily transportable. Rock or stone anchors are generally best suited for places such as a home or community land.

Wood, in the form of cut branches or carved objects, can also hold sufficient energy to be an anchor. Wooden objects have the advantage of having once been alive; they once had energies flowing through them and stored in them and thus adapt to new energies more naturally than other objects. Wooden anchors are very versatile and, depending on the object, can be used for almost any kind of shield. Objects made of other materials (plastic, ceramics, composites, etc.) can be used as anchors, though it may take more work to get them to hold sufficient energy or you may have to charge them more often. However, almost any object can be modified to increase energetic capacity by adding things like sigils, charms, or other customizations. The only things that really don't function as anchors are fragile or easily degradable objects such as cut flowers, herbs, paper, or short-lived plants. Your choice of anchor-to-be is largely a matter of deciding how much effort you want to put into its creation.

The object chosen as an anchor should energetically resonate with the function of the shield. While all shields are protective, some are given additional functions such as grounding, mirroring, energy conversion, filtering, etc. (More in-depth information on various types of shields can be found in resources like *Protection & Reversal Magick* by Jason Miller.) It's best to ensure that the magickal correspondence or

Almost any object can be modified to increase energetic capacity by adding things like sigils, charms, or other customizations. The only things that really don't function as anchors are fragile or easily degradable objects such as cut flowers, herbs, paper, or short-lived plants.

the materials chosen work well with the full purpose of a shield. For example, jet and hematite have a strong correspondence with grounding and protection, making them excellent general shield anchors. However, those same grounding properties would work against the function of a mirror shield and thus shouldn't be used to anchor such a shield. By the same token, an actual mirror would be ideal to use as an anchor for a mirror shield but would be terrible for any shield that doesn't need reflective qualities. A quick flip through your favorite correspondence guide, such as Scott Cunningham's *Encyclopedia of Crystal, Gem & Metal Magic*, will help you make sure your correspondences line up.

Ensuring that your anchor resonates with the person or place being shielded is also critical. For a person, this means making sure your anchor is something they would be comfortable having on their person when needed. If the anchor is a piece of jewelry or a sigil stitched onto clothing, make sure it's something the person would actually want to wear. If the anchor is a stone or other object to be carried, make sure it fits in a pocket or that the person regularly carries a bag with room for it. Further, an object with personal significance will almost always make a better anchor than a new object, regardless of correspondence. For example, a beloved piece of cheap costume jewelry will already be deeply attuned to the bearer in a way that no practitioner could hope to quickly match.

Understanding who is being shielded is just as important in the selection of an anchor as the purpose of the shield. The same holds true for places. An object used to anchor a shield for a specific area, be it a room, building, or parcel of land, should be in harmony with the space. Ideally the object used would come from the place being protected, such as a stone dug from the land, a branch from the garden, and so on. As with objects of significance to a person, objects from the land being protected will usually be better anchors than foreign objects, even if they're not of perfect correspondence. Choosing a potential anchor that is energetically harmonious with the person or place being protected will help the shield to function with maximum efficacy.

The ideal anchor is an object created by the practitioner for that specific purpose. Items such as sigils, charms, talismans, and witch bottles can be specially made to serve as anchors. They can also be added to existing objects so that they better serve as anchors, such as crafting crystals into a talisman or carving sigils in wooden objects. The details of crafting such objects are beyond the scope of this short article, but there are many resources available both on paper and online, such as *Sigil Witchery: A Witch's Guide to Crafting Magick Symbols* by Laura Tempest Zakroff and *Sticks, Stones, Roots & Bones* by Stephanie Rose Bird.

Charging and Maintaining an Anchor

Once an object has been selected to serve as an anchor, it must be charged. If you have experience charging magickal objects, such as charms or talismans, then the process should already be familiar: concentrate on your intent, raise power, and channel that power into the soon-to-be anchor. In this case, your intent is to power a shield for a specific amount of time, usually one month or one week. Power can be raised in many ways, so use whichever method you're most comfortable with. If you don't have a preferred method, a repeated chant, sung aloud with increasing volume on each repetition until your voice strains, is a common way of doing so. The easiest way to transfer the energy you've raised is to pick up the object when the energy peaks and visualize the energy being pulled into the object by a vortex. When the object is full of energy, you should be able to perceive it as a slight blurring of your third eye, an almost staticky feeling when you touch the object, and/or an extra weight when you pick it up. Once fully charged, your anchor is primed and ready to be attached to a shield.

Compared to charging the anchor, casting and attaching the shield is fairly easy. If the shield is for a person, have that person hold the charged anchor; if it's for a place, set the anchor in the center of that space. Cast the shield in your preferred manner, having it fully encase its target: completely surrounding the person or bordering the entire space, including floors and ceilings. You can use the standard bubble shield described earlier as a generic base for your shield. As you fully set the shield, touch the anchor and visualize threads of energy spinning off multiple points of the shield and the center of the anchor to form two tails made of multiple energetic threads. Visualize these two tails of threads spinning together like threads of yarn to form a single strong cord. As you've already set the intent of the energy in the anchor and the intent of the shield to match, these two should naturally want to join together and will become one quite easily. Congratulations, you have now made an anchored shield!

An anchored shield must be periodically recharged, either at appointed intervals or more frequently as the energy becomes depleted. Thankfully this process is identical to that used for the initial charge: set your intent, raise energy, then transfer that energy into the anchor. Before recharging, you should check your anchor for energetic wear and tear. A well-crafted anchor can last for many years, but hard use or less-than-ideal materials can make them wear down over time. This results in the anchor having trouble storing power or a general weakening of the shield. If you find that your shields are not holding up quite as well as they once did, it may be time for a new anchor.

> **An anchored shield must be periodically recharged… Thankfully this process is identical to that used for the initial charge: set your intent, raise energy, then transfer that energy into the anchor.**

Dispelling an Anchor

As your life changes over time, you may find the need to dispel long-term anchored shields. Perhaps you're moving to a new home, gifting the object that previously served as an anchor to a new owner, or perhaps your previous anchor has simply given you its metaphysical all and it's time for a replacement. To dispel an anchored shield, begin by strongly visualizing the shield until you can perceive its energies, usually as light or a feeling of static electricity. Once you can perceive the energy of the shield, formally thank the shield for its service and the protection it has given. Then visualize that energy slowly dissipating into the earth and being grounded. Do the same for the anchor itself. Once both the shield and the energies in the anchor have been fully grounded, thank them again and state that the shield's purpose has been served and its time ended. If you wish, you can then cleanse and purify the former anchor so it can be repurposed.

Anchored shields are a tool that should be in the repertoire of all practitioners. They allow for the creation of long-term shields that can protect people or places without requiring the constant attention of the practitioner placing them. Further, these shields can be sustained almost indefinitely with easy regular maintenance and without unduly draining the caster. Whether they protect a person moving through the world or create an energetic safe haven in a place, anchored shields belong in your practice.

Emily Carlin *is a Witch, writer, teacher, mediator, and ritual presenter based in Seattle, Washington. She currently teaches one-on-one online and at in-person events on the West Coast. For more information and links to her blogs, go to https://about.me/ecarlin.*

Illustrator: Rik Olson

Dirty Magic: Tapping the Power of Found Objects

Lexa Olick

Growing up, my sister became a pro at hunting for four-leaf clovers. At one time she had nearly fifty in her collection, and as her little sister, I was eager to catch up. Sometimes we would hunt together. I quickly trained my eye to spot the only four-leafer in a clover patch. Once I was on a swing set and noticed a lucky charm between my feet. Four-leaf clovers really do just jump out at you once you get into the swing of things.

My sister was a little luckier than I was. She could find clovers with five, six, seven, or even eight leaves. Traditionally,

Traditionally, the leaves of a clover represent faith, hope, and love, so it is the fourth leaf that makes it a symbol of luck....Some people believe the fifth leaf represents wealth and the sixth leaf represents fame. I like to believe that one of the leaves represents intuition.

the leaves of a clover represent faith, hope, and love, so it is the fourth leaf that makes it a symbol of luck. It's trickier to find the meaning behind further leaflets, but some people believe the fifth leaf represents wealth and the sixth leaf represents fame. I like to believe that one of the leaves represents intuition. I may be onto something, because whenever I come across one lucky clover, there is always another one nearby.

What did my sister and I do with our lucky clovers after we found them? We pressed them, of course. I kept these treasures inside another object I thought was of value: a Mickey Mouse notebook my father had purchased for me during a family trip to Disneyland. The notebook was sold at the hotel gift shop. It was protected behind a locked glass case, which allowed my childlike imagination to believe it was as valuable as a leather-bound journal with gold trim pages. In actuality, the journal is soft plastic and still has remnants of the price sticker on the back (fifteen dollars). So while it doesn't have any monetary value, it's still priceless when it comes to sentimental worth. I think of my father whenever I see it.

My sister and I are now adults, but we both managed to keep our lucky clover collection intact. I don't look at the collection often, but the thought of separating the clovers to use for crafts or talismans just doesn't feel right. Their history, symbolism, and age could certainly wield some powerful magic, but I like keeping the collection exactly as it has been for the last thirty years. That cheap plastic notebook, and all the memories and lucky charms inside, are safe.

However, I'm still captivated by the thought of returning to a favorite pastime. As responsibilities pile up and life becomes more complicated, it's harder to steal a moment with nature. Sitting in the middle of a clover patch with the hope of finding the one oddity in the bunch is an undertaking where you're extremely focused in nature, but at the same time it is an activity that allows your mind to relax. You breathe in fresh air and explore a part of nature that normally goes unnoticed when you're just walking from one space to another. However, your mind can relax because you're not inspecting each clover and their leaves individually. Instead, you rake your fingers through the clover and train your eye to spot the difference. For an activity that requires attention to detail, it's very simple and tranquil.

Every now and then, my sister and I reminisce about the clover patch, believing the only reason we haven't found any lucky clovers as adults is because we no longer have the time to spend hours hunting for that elusive fourth leaf. I may have glanced at clover patches on and off throughout my adulthood, but it has probably been about twenty years since I've actually seen a four-leaf clover out in the wild.

We recently bought my father a rollator so he can continue to enjoy his favorite pastime, which is gardening. A rollator is like a walker with wheels, but it also has a folding seat that you can sit or kneel on. He's faced numerous rough patches in his life, and gardening has actually helped him regain some of his strength, for which I am grateful. He normally gardens with my mother, but I've been helping more and more. One of the unexpected benefits is that I've been able to return to the clover patches where I've had success before when it comes to finding four-leaf clovers.

The task seemed fruitless at first. My father showed me where the lucky clover patch was originally, but there wasn't much of it left. The clover had shrunk over the years. Pots, barrels, and stone pavers slowly ate away the lush, green patches. It's sad to think that one day it will disappear completely. I checked other parts of the yard, but I still couldn't locate a single four-leaf clover anywhere.

However, as I was searching, my father started to tell me stories of my brother looking through the clover patch. That caught my attention, because I always associated my sister with the four-leaf clover patch. My brother passed away when I was very young, and it just never occurred to me that he had liked collecting the lucky charms too. I always knew the garden was important to my father for its low-impact exercise, the bushels of blueberries and other fruits, and the satisfaction of seeing what once was dirt blossom into lush rainbows of colors. The care and nurturing of a garden is rewarded with such sensory pleasure, but the growth doesn't stop at plant life. There's history in the dirt. Family memories, chitchats with the neighbors, sharing the crop with friends, or even sharing the crop with furry friends who help themselves to the treats at night all become a part of the earth.

After my father shared his memories of my brother in the garden, I knew I had to find one more four-leaf clover so I could make him a special memento. The symbol of luck would not only be something that had been grown in his own garden but also be a reminder of his family. Plus, it would be such a magical thought that the lucky four-leaf clover patch had survived and continued to grow after all these years. That patch of the garden would have a magical history of fifty years.

I came up with nothing all summer, but finally, at the very end of August, I found the elusive four-leaf clover. It looked exactly as I remembered. The leaves aren't perfectly even. The fourth leaf is tiny and curls easily over the other leaves. I knew that if I had found one four-leaf clover, there was another nearby. After not having any luck finding a single four-leaf clover for twenty years, it took only one magical summer day to find thirty-five. Most importantly, I found the clover in the same lucky patch that my siblings had searched in as children. So even as the clover patch slowly grows smaller, the memories and magic are still alive.

The clovers were small and immediately started to curl and shrivel in my hand. That's why it's a good idea to bring a book with you, so you can press the clover right away. I almost didn't make it to a notebook in time. Pressing the clover removes the moisture from the plant and makes it easier to store. Usually I like to give plants a proper rinse so they're free of dirt. Unfortunately, that is not possible with a fragile item like clover. The delicate little leaflets would most likely fall off or curl into a ball, making it impossible to press. However, the texture, appearance, and even presence of dirt can become a valuable part of a talisman or keepsake. Dust and scratches are visible signs of age and wear, and dirt is a visible sign of an object's origins. These visible, and sometimes tangible, traits remind us that these objects have a past.

The texture, appearance, and even presence of dirt can become a valuable part of a talisman or keepsake. Dust and scratches are visible signs of age and wear, and dirt is a visible sign of an object's origins.

When it comes to clover, the lucky fourth leaf is actually caused by a gene mutation. It is a recessive trait that occurs in white clover plants. However, environmental factors also play a role. The quality of the soil, whether it's well-fertilized soil or soil that's been exposed to certain chemicals, is also believed to cause this mutation.

There's certainly something special in the soil beneath that specific clover patch in my father's garden. It definitely has a rich history of children hunting for four-leaf clovers and being rewarded with the lucky charms. The dirt signifies my father's garden and all the magic that's grown from it. Dirt spots and bug bites don't diminish the value of the four-leaf clover. In fact, the flaws further illustrate the clover's story and add more meaning to a talisman.

Cleansing an Object

Normally we cleanse an object before ritual use to remove any negative energy. That's especially important when you don't know where the object originated from. With found objects, or objects purchased secondhand, there's a chance that the previous owner was filled with negativity or that the object wasn't handled, stored, or transported with the greatest care. Here are some quick ways to cleanse an object.

Salt Water Soak

Fill a nonporous bowl with salt water and completely immerse your object in the water. Let it sit for a few hours or overnight. If you don't want to completely submerge the object in water, fill a spray bottle with salt water and gently mist it. You can also dip your fingertips into the bowl and sprinkle the water over your object. Afterward, you can set the object aside to air-dry, or gently pat the object dry with a cloth so you don't scrub or scour away any markings.

Running Water

The quickest way to cleanse an object is to hold it underneath running water. Don't scrub away at the object with your fingers or a sponge. Simply let the water run over the object.

Burn Incense

Choose your favorite cleansing incense, such as sage. Light the incense and wait for the smoke to settle into a nice, steady flow. It shouldn't take long. Run the object through the smoke, making sure the smoke makes contact with every part of the object. The smoke will clear away any unwanted energy. This method even works on spaces.

Candle Flame

Light a white candle, or a candle of another color if it's more conducive to your goal. Carefully hold your object and wave it over the candle flame. Do not use this method if your object is flammable. Cloth, herbs, or paper items are obviously not suitable.

Besom Sweep

Place your object in front of you. Hold your besom (a traditional broom) in your hands and sweep away the negativity. Do not sweep the besom back and forth. Instead, use slow and gentle sweeping motions to pull negativity out from your object and cast them away. Sweep the besom outward. This method is perfect for fragile items or items that may be flammable. I like this method for cleansing cloth dolls, because other methods with dirt, salt, smoke, or any type of dampness can harm the fabric or seep into the stuffing.

Bury

Dirt and salt absorb the negative energy from an object. Bury your object in the earth or within a bowl of salt and let it sit for several hours or overnight. Retrieve your object and shake it free of any debris or rinse it with water. I especially like this method for cleansing crystals or candles. However, if your object is plastic, I recommend burying it in dirt instead of salt. Sometimes salt can eat away at the plastic and leave behind scratches. While that's the sort of wear and tear I like to see in my found objects, I prefer the wear and tear to happen organically and over time.

BELLS

Sound and vibrations break up and dispel bad energies. Hold a bell over your object and ring it back and forth. This is a great method for fragile or delicate objects because it requires very little handling. Flammable objects, such as dried herbs, pressed flowers, or cloth, can be safely cleansed with a ringing bell. It's also useful for cleansing jewelry because certain metals and stones can react to smoke, water, or salt.

If I'm making something like sage wands, I always wash the pieces of sage before I bundle them. That way, they're free of dirt when it comes time for smudging. However, clovers are too delicate to rinse and the dirt is a part of their magic. I may clean and cleanse tools for ritual use, but certain objects only need to be cleansed spiritually. I personally like creating talismans that show their age. I'm impressed by something that can survive for so long. Since talismans are worn to enhance personal power, the dirt and scrapes tell an intimate story that can only inspire more power from the talisman.

I cleanse away the bad energy but never wash away the magic.

DIY Found-Object Talisman

We carry energy, just as the stones we wear carry energy. Found pebbles are elements of Earth. They are ageless and symbolize endless strength and protection. They communicate with us silently. We feel the stone's strength and stability when we hold it in our hands. Wear this talisman as a reminder of your connection to Earth and use it to draw strength. It will instill confidence in its wearer.

No cleaning is required for this project! To begin, all you need is a mini glass vial pendant. These look like tiny vials, usually with a cork, and can be strung onto a necklace. The vials are sold at any store that sells jewelry findings, but you can substitute it with a floating locket if that's easier to obtain. The rest of the materials you can find as you go. Let nature influence your choices! Then when you look back at your talisman, you'll see that it tells a story.

SUPPLIES

- 1 mini glass vial charm

- 1 small pebble

- Other small item(s) of your choosing to place in the vial, such as a feather, an eggshell, a seed, etc. (optional)

- Soil from the area where you procured your pebble

- A cord or chain

Step One

Accept the next opportunity that comes along to be fully immersed in nature, even if it's a simple stroll outside. Clear your mind and admire the beauty and natural influences around you. Hopefully, during your stroll, there will be something that calls out to you. Sometimes a single pebble out of a group of many will distinguish itself from the others. For example, a pebble with the tiniest fleck that catches the sun and looks like glitter might catch your eye. Along the way, you may also find a fallen feather, an eggshell, or even a dandelion seed. If you open yourself up to receiving these gifts, something will call out to you. Keep in mind that your pebble and any other items you find should be small enough to fit inside the vial. You can fill the vial with as many found items as you like.

Step Two

Once you find that special pebble, hold it in your right hand and place your left hand on the ground where you discovered it. Feel your energy connect to the energy of the Earth. Take deep breaths and concentrate on that connection.

Step Three

Gather a small amount of dirt from the exact spot where you found your pebble. You don't need much, so you can probably just use your fingers or a spoon. Now place the dirt in the vial. Feel each speck of dirt fall from your fingertips and into the vial. The dirt is a part of the pebble's history, and including it in the vial will allow the Earth and the pebble to strengthen each other's energy. Think about the balance of nature and how everything in nature is made of energy and shares a connection. We are all connected to the soil, just as the pebble is connected to the soil.

Step Four

Offer your thanks to the Earth and then drop the pebble into the vial and on top of the dirt. If you found any other items that spoke to you, you can now add them to the vial as well.

Step Five

Use one of the cleansing methods mentioned earlier to cleanse the vial and its contents. I recommend burning sage and letting the smoke hit the vial. You can even direct the smoke into the opening of the vial.

Step Six

Empower the vial with positive energy. Let it sit outside and in direct sunlight for one day. Leave the cork off.

Step Seven

Place the cork in the vial and attach the charm to a cord or chain.

Lexa Olick *is the author of* Witchy Crafts: 60 Enchanted Projects for the Creative Witch *and has contributed to many of the Llewellyn annuals. She is a graduate of the University of Buffalo, where she studied art and art history. Her artistic journey began as a web designer, but her true passions lie in jewelry design and doll making. When she is not writing or crafting, she spends her free time traveling, gardening, and adding to her collection of antique glassware. She currently lives in New York with her family and several hyperactive pets.*

Illustrator: M. Kathryn Thompson

The Magic of Metals

Elizabeth Barrette

Though many people know about stone magic, fewer people know about metal magic. Yet metal has been a part of magic since the beginning. Our ancestors wondered at the shine of silver and gold, and especially the powerful star metal that fell from the sky. Let's take a look at what metal is and what you can do with it.

Metal as an Element

Metal is a magical element in the Eastern system, along with Fire, Earth, Water, and Wood. These exist in a complex, dynamic balance. Each element has a positive relationship with two other elements and a negative relationship with the remaining two. "Earth forms Metal" and "Metal holds Water" are the affinities. "Fire melts Metal" and "Metal chops Wood" are the enmities. If you work with the Eastern set of elements, these relationships advise you on what to do or to avoid in ritual or spellcraft. You can combine Metal with Earth or Water for good results, but Fire or Wood don't mix as well.

Metals also exist as elements on the periodic table in science. This is very useful to know if you like to mix magic and science. The periodic table of elements divides them into alkali metals, alkaline-earth metals (magnesium), transition metals (titanium, niobium, iron, copper, silver, gold, mercury), and post-transition metals (aluminum, tin, lead, bismuth). The inner transition metals have two subgroups, lanthanides (neodymium) and actinides, which are offset from the main body of the periodic table. There are also metalloids (silicon), which have some characteristics of both metals and nonmetals. Elements with similar properties appear near each other on the periodic table. For maximum magical compatibility, follow that pattern.

Classic Metals

The classic metals, or metals of antiquity, are those that people knew about and used in ancient times: gold, silver, copper, tin, iron, lead, and mercury. Our ancestors discovered gold, silver, lead, and copper in prehistoric times. Gold, silver, and copper form nuggets that are easy to identify and work. Lead and tin exist only as ores but are simple to smelt at campfire temperatures. The discovery of tin sparked the Bronze Age, because bronze is an alloy of copper and tin. (An alloy is a mixture of two or more different metals.) People knew about iron but could not smelt it, due to its high melting temperature, until they invented hotter furnaces and the dawn of the Iron Age. Mercury was the last of the classic metals to be discovered, not long before the Common Era.

Gold corresponds to the Sun, Fire, and masculine energy. Naturally yellowish, it can be alloyed with other metals to create white, pink, or green gold. Black Hills gold is famously multicolored in this manner, and its traditional grapevines and other natural motifs make it ideal for magical use. God icons and spiritual jewelry are often made from gold. Cupid's arrows of love are tipped with gold and fletched with dove feathers, making this metal ideal for love magic. Gold also brings wealth and success. As gold is a dominant metal, its alloys generally behave like gold in a magical context, although purer is better if you can afford it. Bear in mind that pure gold is extremely soft, so for most purposes an alloy works better anyway.

God icons and spiritual jewelry are often made from gold. Cupid's arrows of love are tipped with gold and fletched with dove feathers, making this metal ideal for love magic. Gold also brings wealth and success.

Silver corresponds to the Moon, Water, and feminine energy. It has a whitish color and tarnishes to gray, brown, or black. Textured silver jewelry can look fantastic when the lower parts are permitted to tarnish while the upper parts are polished bright, making the design stand out more. Because it is so soft, silver is often alloyed to make it sturdy enough for jewelry. Crescent moon circlets are often made of silver like this. Since this metal also appears in silverware, an old table knife can make an excellent athame. Silver is also the most magically impressionable metal, easy to program with energy but also susceptible to contamination. Storing it in silk helps keep it pristine.

Copper corresponds to Venus, Water, and feminine energy. This soft metal is popular for jewelry, athames, and cauldrons. It is the best

choice for love magic. Copper holds memories well. For this reason I like to collect pressed pennies, the kind you get from a machine that stamps an image on them.

Copper also works well with Fire magic, which not many people know. If you like to throw ritual items into a bonfire to burn, you could also use copper to make these more exciting. Suppose you're used to writing things on a slip of paper. If you use a larger piece of paper, it can be folded around some wood chips and other inclusions to make a more visual impact. A small scoop of colorful fireplace sprinkles will produce rainbow flames. They use copper to make greens and blues, which are colors that our coven saw lots of when we tried this. Another trick we used was saving pieces of green cardboard (copper makes a lot of the blue and green dyes, too), which burned quite well and quite green. We even have a lighter with a copper wire that turns the flame green.

Tin corresponds to Jupiter, Air, and masculine energy. By itself, tin is popular for crafts such as lantern shades. Its superior acoustic qualities make it suitable for musical instruments such as the tin whistle. Because it doesn't oxidize, tin represents permanence and longevity. It also alloys well, making it a good metal for any kind of teamwork.

Iron corresponds to Mars, Fire, and masculine energy. Meteoric iron has the highest magical potency and is less prone to shatter magic, whereas cold iron and steel can break a lot of spells. Many old spells mention using an iron knife or scissors to break a hex or banish a monster.

However, in some contexts iron can contain or channel magic. For example, horseshoes and horseshoe nails are used to attract luck. Most people hang a horseshoe points up, but a blacksmith hangs it points down above his anvil—to pour the energy into his workspace. Magic can also be worked through iron or steel tools, such as sewing needles for embroidered magic.

Risky Metals

Some metals that have magical qualities also have dangerous qualities. Of those appearing in traditional resources, lead and mercury are the most hazardous. For maximum safety, some people choose to avoid these. Aluminum is a very close substitute for mercury in magical contexts, lacking only the liquid quality; a combination of aluminum and silver make a near-perfect match for mercury. Lead is harder to substitute, as it is the only ancient metal corresponding to Earth, but you could try tin or iron instead. Another option is to write their symbols instead of using the materials themselves: mercury (☿) and lead (♄). However, it is still possible to work with the risky metals as long as you take precautions.

Mercury corresponds to Mercury, Air, and masculine energy. It has been used for luck, scrying, and protection, all of which have better alternatives now. But it's also the strongest connection to the god Mercury, which is less substitutable. This metal is easiest to obtain in an old-fashioned thermometer. The metal is sealed inside the glass, so as long as you take care not to break the glass, it's safe—and even has a convenient wand shape. You can seal the thermometer inside a padded case for extra protection and it will still work.

Lead corresponds to Saturn, Earth, and masculine energy. It is grounding and guarding. Cupid's arrows of indifference are tipped with lead and fletched with owl feathers, making it ideal for breaking love magic or bad relationships. Lead is still used for a lot of things such as fishing sinkers, ammunition, and cheap alloys for figurines. It is most toxic when it gets inside the body, but even handling it with bare hands is not a great idea. You can wear gloves while applying a protective coating. Figurines can be made reasonably safe by painting them with craft sealant. Lead weights such as sinkers can be sealed into the core of a wand or other artifact. In fact, one of the safest options is to buy something that already has a lead core—many weighted items are like this. As long as the rest of the material has little or no metal, it shouldn't interfere with the magical qualities of the lead.

Modern Metals

In the Common Era, many more metals have been discovered. Of the 118 elements in the periodic table, about 86 are metals of some sort. A handful of these have notable applications in magic.

Aluminum corresponds to Mercury, Air, and masculine energy. It is cheap and lightweight and enhances mental clarity. It makes a good substitute for mercury. Anodized aluminum takes color beautifully, making it suitable for color magic. Sets of rainbow rings are often made this way and can represent the goddess Iris as well as gay pride.

Bismuth forms rainbow crystals that look like stepped pyramids. It is one of the best focal materials for working with technomagic. It also helps with understanding complexities and doing group work. Because of its coloration, bismuth can stand for Iris or any other rainbow deity.

Magnesium is supremely suited to Fire magic. When you shave it very fine, it forms a powder that burns with a brilliant white-hot light. For this reason, magnesium is often used to make fireworks, of which the ground fountains are among the safer options. You could buy these and use as directed in a ritual context. They look spectacular.

You can buy a magnesium firestarter for camping, which will work even if it has been dropped in water and wiped off. I have used this to start ritual fires with great results. However, be aware that magnesium wants to burn. If you channel Fire energy into it, that tendency gets stronger. So practice on a paved surface until you know how it behaves before you try to use it in ritual. Similarly, a pinch or two of magnesium powder will give a bright silver flame, if bundled into paper and thrown in a fire.

Neodymium is best known for its use in magnets. Rare-earth magnets can be very powerful. I have a set of magnetic spheres that make fantastic fidgets, making a fun clicking or chirping sound as they jump together. When you have a set of these, you can form them into different shapes, such as a square, circle, or pyramid, which makes them very useful for magic. In addition to spheres, magnets come in many shapes, and you can buy a set of high-power magnets at most science stores. There are also levitating pens and wands that function with magnets in the stem or base.

Magnetic magic is all about attraction and repulsion. First write what you want or don't want on one magnet. Then use another magnet to pull it in or push it away. For extra impact, write with a levitating pen.

Magnetic magic is all about attraction and repulsion. First write what you want or don't want on one magnet. Then use another magnet to pull it in or push it away. For extra impact, write with a levitating pen.

Niobium corresponds to Water, particularly tears, as it is named for Niobe. Because of this, niobium helps with grief, particularly the loss of children. This metal can also be tinted with rainbow colors, singly or swirled together. It is very popular in jewelry for this reason. Because of its coloration, niobium can stand for Iris or any other rainbow deity.

Silicon is a metalloid, which, like bismuth, is one of the few elements truly suited to technomagic. Computer chips are made of it, after all! In fact, motherboard is often upcycled into jewelry or boxes, which are ideal for technomagic.

Titanium corresponds to Air. It is light but strong, which makes it an ideal metal for cultivating resilience. Some surgical implants and many adaptive devices are made from it, so it also suits healing magic. Because canes have been used as magic staves or wands, a titanium one can be quite powerful. Like niobium, titanium can also be tinted in bright colors, single or mixed. Because of its color potential and medical safety, titanium is very popular in jewelry. Similarly, it can stand for Iris or any other rainbow deity.

Alloys

Alloys are mixtures of two or more different metals. Each one has its own unique set of strengths and weaknesses. While they can be similar to one parent metal—alloys of gold and silver really tend to act like those metals—sometimes they're quite different in color and behavior. Two of the most common alloys are bronze and brass.

Bronze is an alloy of copper and tin. Where copper is pinkish and tin is nearly white, bronze has a dark yellowish to brownish color. The acoustic qualities of tin carry over though, making bronze very popular for bells and other musical instruments. It is also one of the most popular materials for high-quality devotional statues. Some jewelry is made of bronze, especially for men.

Brass is an alloy of copper and zinc. Where copper is pinkish and zinc is whitish or greenish, brass has a bright yellowish color barely darker than gold, so it is often used as a substitute for gold. Brass makes lovely statues. While it can be used for jewelry, it is notorious for turning green—and even turning your skin green. Like bronze, brass is used for musical instruments, and indeed a whole orchestral section (the horns) is called the "brass."

Metals in Astrology

The classic metals, and some modern ones, have associations with the heavens. You can use these metals or their symbols to represent the planets or attune other objects to that energy. Conveniently, most of these symbols are easy to find in magical jewelry, and you can also carve or paint them on ritual tools.

Some people like to keep an astrological set of statues depicting the planets or their ruling deities, or other objects with symbolic colors. In cases where the metal is not used for statuary, substitutes may be made, such as aluminum instead of mercury. I went with a set of planetary glasses myself, so I can always have an astrologically appropriate chalice if I need one.

These are the classic metals and their heavenly bodies:

Gold corresponds to the **Sun:** ☉

Silver corresponds to the **Moon:** ☽

Mercury corresponds to **Mercury:** ☿

Copper corresponds to **Venus:** ♀

Iron corresponds to **Mars:** ♂

Tin corresponds to **Jupiter:** ♃

Lead corresponds to **Saturn:** ♄

Extending beyond this list, we find modern correspondences such as these:

Zinc corresponds to **Uranus:** ♅

Cobalt corresponds to **Neptune:** ♆

Bismuth corresponds to **Pluto:** ♇

Earth is sometimes associated with lead, but lead already corresponds to Saturn. To derive a unique metal for Earth, we may consider silicon, which is the most common metalloid in the planetary crust:

Silicon corresponds to **Earth:** ⊕

Metalworking

Things you make for yourself hold some of your personal energy. They are more powerful magical tools because of this. People use metal to make many decorative or practical items.

Gold, silver, and copper are easy to work. Gold is too expensive for most people. Silver is pricey, but you can get a lot of jewelry pieces at somewhat affordable prices. I like silver for making magical artifacts because it's soft and holds energy very well. Copper is cheap, including copper wire for sculpture or jewelry. Craft foil is often copper or brass, and sometimes tin, for tracing or punching patterns. Copper or brass pipe makes an excellent wand, and you can stuff things inside it.

Colored metals—anodized aluminum, niobium, titanium—are easy to find, and prices vary but are usually affordable. You do need rubber-tipped tools to avoid scratching them. Start with aluminum if you can. Titanium is sturdy stuff and requires more strength to bend. These metals are among my favorites for color magic when I'm not just using stones.

> **Gold, silver, and copper are easy to work.... I like silver for making magical artifacts because it's soft and holds energy very well.... Copper or brass pipe makes an excellent wand, and you can stuff things inside it.**

Bronze can be worked in various ways that require only modest skills, such as bending or stamping. More adventurous crafters may wish to explore advanced sculpture with casting molten bronze into a mold. There are people crafting gorgeous Pagan statues now. A model is made and used to create a mold from which many castings can be made.

Iron has the highest melting point, which makes it demanding but rewarding to use. You can buy "blank" knife blades to mount with a handle and sharpen, which is as close as most people will get to making their own athame. A few people take blacksmith classes and learn to forge metal. One of the first apprentice projects is usually a candleholder, making this craft highly relevant for Pagans who want a challenge. Trivets are another popular project. I have two pentacles and another trivet with brooms on it. Another option for adventurous crafters is welding, useful in creating large-scale tools or sculptures. I have seen some very Pagan garden art made from upcycled iron bits welded together. One local crafter makes astrolabes.

. . . .

Metal underlies much of human civilization and many forms of magic. Each metal has its own strengths and weaknesses. Some are more practical, others more decorative. They all have their own set of correspondences for things like heavenly bodies, deities, elements, gender, and the type of spells or rituals they best suit. They make many of our magical tools. As you work with metals, you can build up a set of those you like and learn what they do for you.

Elizabeth Barrette *has been involved with the Pagan community for more than thirty years. She served as managing editor of* PanGaia *for eight years and dean of studies at the Grey School of Wizardry for four years. She has written columns on beginning and intermediate Pagan practice, Pagan culture, and Pagan leadership. Her book* Composing Magic: How to Create Magical Spells, Rituals, Blessings, Chants, and Prayers *explains how to combine writing and spirituality. She lives in central Illinois, where she has done much networking with Pagans in her area, such as coffeehouse meetings and open sabbats. Her other public activities include Pagan picnics and science fiction conventions. She enjoys magical crafts, historic religions, and gardening for wildlife. Her other writing fields include speculative fiction, gender studies, and social and environmental issues. Visit her blog,* The Wordsmith's Forge *(https://ysabetwordsmith.dreamwidth.org/), or her website,* PenUltimate Productions *(http://penultimateproductions. weebly.com/). Her coven site, which includes extensive Pagan materials, is* Greenhaven Tradition *(http://greenhaventradition.weebly.com/).*

Illustrator: Bri Hermanson

Witchcraft Essentials

PRACTICES, RITUALS & SPELLS

Make Your Own Witch Tools: Cheap & Easy Ways to Stock Your Altar

Ari & Jason Mankey

Athames, censers, chalices…The tools of Witchcraft often seem mysterious and expensive, but the most common ones are most likely already in your house! Better yet, those tools don't have to be ornate or attention-grabbing. The vast majority look like everyday items and generally don't elicit a first or even a second glance. A full altar of ritual tools is easy to put together and won't cost you much more than twenty dollars (and often less).

When I (Jason) discovered Witchcraft, I was a poor college student with very little discretionary income. In order to put together a working altar full of ritual tools, I scoured my kitchen and thrift stores to find what I needed. Ari, on the other hand, discovered Witchcraft in high school, and not only didn't have much money for her tools but also had to keep her practice of the Craft a secret from her mother! We've replaced many of our tools over the years, but some of our earliest and simplest tools remain a vital part of our Witchcraft practice.

For many Witches, their most important "tool" is their altar, the spot where they store many of their most magickal items and do the work of Witchcraft. Any flat surface will work as an altar, and some of the easiest to use in our home are the tops of bookshelves and dressers. Not only are these spots nice and flat, but they are known to attract knickknacks and are often in bedrooms where they won't be bothered. When Ari began her practice, her first altar was a foldable piece of black cardboard. In the middle of the night, while the sister she shared a bedroom with was fast asleep, she'd light candles and work magick on that altar, unbeknownst to the rest of her family. (If you do use a cardboard altar, be especially careful when putting lit candles on it!)

A traditional athame is a double-sided knife with a wooden handle used for directing energy, but any old knife will work, and for this reason both of us worked with athames very early on as Witches. As someone who has always enjoyed spending time in the kitchen, my first athame was simply a favorite carving knife. After a trip home to visit my parents, I picked up an old pocket knife from my time in the Boy Scouts and used that as an athame off and on for several years.

Ari's first athame was far more elaborate than anything I used but was also extremely nondescript. She simply went out and purchased a lovely (though inexpensive) letter opener, and it's a tool she still uses today. Quartz points, such as ones that might end up on a necklace, are also great for directing energy and can be used as an athame. Wands are just as good as athames for directing energy and are easy to acquire. Wands made from fallen tree branches are often the first tools of many Witches!

Chalice is just a fancy name for a cup, and most of us have a dozen "chalices" just sitting in our kitchens. Without really realizing it, we often grow attached to certain cups and mugs, and when we grow an attachment to something, it usually makes for a great magickal tool. (All of us have had a favorite coffee cup or two fall to the ground and break— remember how upsetting that was?) Do you have a wine drinker in the house? A piece of stemware makes for a great chalice simply because of the way it looks.

The pentacle, generally a pentagram on a disc used to bless and consecrate magickal items, is often one of the most difficult to find and/or cobble together tools for many Witches. However, there are still some quick and simple ways to come up with a pentagram on the fly. The easiest method is to draw a five-pointed star on a paper plate with a marker or pen. (If you want to make it extra fancy, you can "draw" the star by dripping candle wax onto the paper plate.) There are other common household items you can use here too. An apple turned on its side and cut in the middle will reveal a five-pointed star in the center. Such a pentacle can be used only once, but it makes for a great offering at the end of ritual.

Most of us have decorative items in our homes that make for great pentacles too. Star-shaped Christmas ornaments, many of which are nice and flat, work well and don't attract all that much attention. My parents always decorated at least one of the bathrooms in our house with seashells and sand dollars, and sand dollars are well known for the five-pointed star visible on one side.

One of Ari's most prized magickal items is a terracotta bowl given to her by a friend in high school, only she's never used it as a bowl. Instead she's always used it as a cauldron to recharge and refresh her magickal items, such as stones and jewelry. (Cauldrons are places of rebirth after all!) The lid on the cauldron is a star-shaped Christmas ornament that also doubles as a pentacle. Need a cauldron that will stand up to heat? Kitchen pots work in a pinch, as do ramekins designed for desserts such as crème brûlée.

I marked out my first magick circles with tealight candles, but what if you are in a location where you can't light candles or simply aren't allowed to? An easy and inexpensive way to designate your sacred space is with a braided ribbon laid out in a circle. As a bonus, if other people see the ribbon, most of them will have no idea what it's for.

An easy and inexpensive way to designate your sacred space is with a braided ribbon laid out in a circle. As a bonus, if other people see the ribbon, most of them will have no idea what it's for.

Need to do some magick in a pinch and lack the proper supplies? Birthday candles are great for spellwork, and they burn quickly, releasing their energy out into the universe in a hurry. No access to tarot cards and need to do a little divination? Any necklace with a magickal charm or a quartz point attached to it will make an effective pendulum.

Most Witches keep four items representative of earth, air, water, and fire on their altars. These items are often chosen for their usefulness. Water and salt (for earth) mixed together is an especially useful combination for cleansing spaces, items, and oneself. Other times, items representative of the elements are placed on the altar simply because of the energies they give off and add to our magickal work.

Often the items we use to represent the elements are obvious, such as a small dish of water for water, a candle for fire, salt or rocks for earth, and incense for air. But there are other alternatives. My earliest altars included fallen leaves to represent air, while Ari used a wooden flute. An item symbolizing the power of fire can be more than just a conventional candle. Any metal item created in the fires of a forge will work, as will dried hot peppers (probably my favorite way to represent fire!). Electric candles are easy to get these days, look almost like the real thing, and never have to be blown out.

Salt is easy enough to get, but there are other easily obtainable things out there to represent the power of earth. Flour and rice from the pantry work well, as do dirt, rocks, and sand collected from your yard, a local park, or a lake/ocean shore. Small bowls and dishes from the kitchen make perfect containers for whatever you use to represent the element of earth and to hold water.

Most Witches use incense (or some other burning matter such as sage) and salted water to cleanse their ritual spaces, but sometimes those just aren't an option. If the risk of fire is an issue where you live, a few drops of essential oil in a spray bottle full of water will both cleanse and purify your ritual space. Don't have access to much in the way of essential oils? Check to see if there's some peppermint extract in the kitchen spice rack. A spritz or two of your favorite perfume or cologne will work here too, especially if those scents conjure up positive feelings.

Among our most prized possessions are the various deity statues we have scattered over the various altars in our house. Deity statues can provide a source of focus during rituals and magickal activities and help facilitate stronger relationships with deity. They are often expensive, but luckily there are several great alternatives. My first Horned God "statue" was a pinecone I found in an apartment complex, and Ari's first Goddess statue was a statue of the Virgin Mary she got as a gift from her Catholic grandmother. If an item or image connects you to a deity, then it'll make for a great "statue."

Statues can also be a bit tongue in cheek. With Legos you can build a deity almost exactly as you see it in your mind's eye! Action figures make great "statues" too, and I'll admit to having a few on my altar over the years.

Tools don't have to be fancy or cost a lot of money. What makes a tool work is our belief that it will work! If you are comfortable with whatever it is you are using, it will work for you. Witches tend to be practical folk, and using things that are already hanging around the house or yard is the height of practicality. Happy spellcasting!

Ari Mankey *has been practicing Witchcraft and creating spells for over twenty years. Away from the Craft, she has devoted her life to medical laboratory science and developing the perfect whisky ice cream.*

Jason Mankey *has written six books for Llewellyn, including* Transformative Witchcraft: The Greater Mysteries, Witch's Wheel of the Year: Rituals for Circles, Solitaries & Covens, *and* Llewellyn's Little Book of Yule, *and is a frequent speaker and teacher at Pagan festivals across North America. He and Ari lead two covens in California's Bay Area, where they live with their two cats, Summer and Evie.*

Illustrator: Tim Foley

A Little Smudge of Magic

Charlie Rainbow Wolf

Magic seems to be very popular these days, doesn't it? Go into any hippie shop, online marketplace, or even some of the high street chain stores, and you will see an assortment of magical accoutrements. There's nothing new about magic; people from all cultures have been using fetishes and other charmed objects for centuries. But perhaps these days it's more accessible.

I've known people to be a bit wary of magic, but it's been my experience that it's because they don't really understand it. Let's face it: the core of anything supernatural is simply something we don't understand, and it's easy to fear the unknown. In my mind, there is no difference between the herbs in a smudge pot and the incense in a thurible.

A Smudge of History

The use of herbs goes back to the dawn of time, for these were the natural remedies the ancestors sought when someone needed healing or something needed cleaning or purifying. Over time it was found that different plants were more suitable for some purposes than others. So-called modern medicine may feel that we've outgrown this, yet even today, a study published in the *Journal of Ethnopharmacology* shows that certain smokes, when burned for an hour, have the potential to eradicate 94 percent of bacteria from the air (Shekhar et al.).

If you're new to smudge, you might think it's limited to the white sage bundled into sticks, but it's important to remember that all plants have their own energy signature and their own beneficial properties. Many of them can be used when smudging. What makes a plant good for smudge use depends on many things, including its magical properties, its healing essences, and whether it smells pleasant or not when burned.

My personal history with smudge goes back to approximately half my lifetime. Yes, there were times when I denied how important it was to me, times when I could only smudge outside because the smell panicked the dog, but I somehow always returned to the sacred smoke. Now I try to start all my days with my own simple smudge ceremony. Mostly I use simple white sage, adding different herbs or resins if I'm smudging for a specific purpose. My smudge pot is one my daughter made in high school. It looks awkward and some might even say ugly, but it connects me to her and to all the ancestors who stand behind me.

Before Smudging

Smudging is not hard. Smudge is just smoldering plant matter. It cannot in and of itself solve a problem, heal an ailment, or fix your life. What it *can* do, though, is give your thoughts a focal point for working on these issues—and as we all know, real magic begins in the mind.

> **[Smudge] cannot in and of itself solve a problem, heal an ailment, or fix your life. What it *can* do, though, is give your thoughts a focal point for working on these issues— and as we all know, real magic begins in the mind.**

One of the most important concepts to embrace when you start to smudge is to realize that everything is energy. This theory is practiced by many cultures, and if you've ever seen the Netflix series *Tidying Up with Marie Kondo*, you have watched her kneel in a home and connect with its energy before she starts her work. It's important to connect with the space you are going to smudge so you resonate with the area before you light your herbs.

Now, this next part might sound a bit crazy, but before you smudge yourself, you also have to make sure you're connected with yourself. This is because you don't just have a physical body made up of muscles and organs and bones; you also have a subtle body made up of energy. Your physical body is the chassis for your subtle body, and your subtle body is what makes up your personality and animates your physical body. The two have to work in harmony or there will be an imbalance, a dis-ease.

The subtle body can be seen as the seven layers of energy that surround your physical body, each one blending into the other. The etheric layer is the one that sits right on top of your physical body, and it is followed by the emotional layer, then the mental, astral, etheric template, celestial, and, finally, causal layer—the outermost vibration of the subtle body. Different practices may have different names for the layers, but the energy is the same, and this is what some psychics read or what many healers work with when they say they are studying your aura. All living things have some kind of an energy field that can be seen as an aura.

Have you ever walked into a room where two people had been arguing and you could feel the thickness and discomfort in the air? Have you ever entered a church or other spiritual place and immediately felt uplifted and at peace with things? Buildings and other structures hang on to energy, and even though they don't have their own living aura, they do absorb the vibrations of what has happened around them. A healthy diet isn't just about what you put in your mouth, but also involves what you feed your mind and your spirit. Smudging your surroundings keeps them fresh.

A Bit about Energy

For the purpose of this article, *energy* is the unique resonances you're going to be working with: your own unique vitality and the vibrational essence of the plants in your smudge. It's this marriage that allows the energy flow to work through you, bringing harmony to yourself and the area you're smudging. The energy flows through your subtle body to influence your physical body.

Energy work is a broad term that covers many different techniques from many different cultures and customs. Because you're working with energy signatures when you smudge, it's possible to blend smudging with other practices. Smudging works by bringing your essence into balance by ensuring that your subtle body and your physical body are working in harmony. When the subtle body is whole, it opens the door for the physical body to find its wholeness.

The benefits of smudging are especially potent when associated with ritual. Use smudge before an event as preparation for the site, or to clear the energies and bring a close to things after the ceremony has taken place. In the past, I've smudged people as they entered the sacred space before an esbat or a sabbat. I have smudged houses before new owners took up residency, and smudged tools that were obtained secondhand to remove any residue that might still be on them from the previous owner. The most important aspect of smudging is your attitude. Intention is everything. It's the combination of your state of mind and the herbs you're using that will define the purpose of your smudging—and influence the outcome too.

A Smudge More about Energy Medicine

Medicine does not always mean prescribed pills and potions from the pharmacist. In many cultures, *medicine* is the word used to describe the energy just discussed. I've mentioned my belief that every living thing has an energy signature. Herbal medicine considers what the energy of a specific plant has to offer to a particular condition.

My Cherokee friends talk about their medicine wheel and their medicine animals. In this case, the wheel is a place of energy and balance, and the animal's medicine is the qualities it embodies and the lessons that can be learned from observing it. The medicine belonging to something— or indeed, someone, in the case of a medicine person or healer—is not innately good or bad; it's how it's used that makes it so. Good medicine makes us feel whole and balanced, while bad medicine makes us feel awkward and distressed.

One of the greatest benefits of smudging is that it sets the tone for the work I'm about to do. It allows my mind to go to that place of creativity and confidence. The mind is very powerful, and our outlook has a strong influence on whether we succeed or fail. The brain is full of neuroreceptors that carry information to the mind, and they will focus on what the mind tells them to find. You have to train your mind to communicate with your psyche, or you won't reach your goals. Many of those who preach about the law of attraction fail to realize that you have to train your mind to communicate with your psyche or you won't reach your goals.

Before You Smudge

Whenever you do anything for the first time—especially when it concerns something magical or ceremonial—it's special and perhaps even sacred to you. Understand that this also applies to your first smudge.

Even if you have smudged in the past, approaching it with new information and insight brings a new perspective—potentially a far more profound one. It's worth taking your time so you can assimilate every aspect of the smudging experience.

You don't need all the bells and whistles that you sometimes see sold with smudge kits. If you want to incorporate them, fine. There's absolutely no reason not to. But they're the jam on the toast, not the loaf of bread. All you really need is a heatproof container and a combustion briquette (a charcoal disc, as is used for loose incense, will suffice), your chosen herbs, and the smoke that those herbs create.

Ignite your fuel source (I use a charcoal disc; they're inexpensive and readily available) and put it in the bottom of your smudge pot. Be careful when you do this. Use tongs or a similar utensil, for it will get hot quickly and you don't want to burn your fingers. Get it good and glowing before you add your herbs. As you do this, think about how fire itself is a cleansing element, burning and purifying. Thank the fire for its presence and for being there for you to light your smudge.

When the disc is glowing, it's time to add the smudge. Take a good pinch or even a small scoop of herbs and slowly—keeping your intention focused in your mind—sprinkle them onto the hot charcoal. Remember, you're not lighting them. You don't want to see flames; you want to see the smoke that comes from them as they smolder. If they start to flare up, add a bit more to reduce the available oxygen to the flames. If you have to blow out the flames to get them smoking, that's okay too.

Congratulations! You're ready to smudge!

Area Cleansing with Smudge

This is often the first type of smudging that people think of. If you're clearing the energies in your home or some other building or type of surroundings, simply get your smudge burning and then walk around the area, taking care that you get the smoke into all areas from the ground level upward, and into all corners, cracks, and crevices. As you do so, make sure you're focusing on the purpose of your smudge. The smoke and your thoughts will do the rest.

Smudging isn't limited to buildings. I regularly smudge the yarden (yard + garden = yarden) before the growing season, again in late summer, and also in the winter, when nature seems to be sleeping. If you have a ritual space and want to clear the area before a gathering, smudge it. There's no limit to where or when you can smudge; just be sure that you're not violating any fire codes with your smoke and that no one in attendance is allergic to the herbs or sensitive to smoke!

Your Personal Smudge

This is the second part of my daily smudge routine. After I've smudged my house and my studio, I smudge myself. It's kind of like yoga with smoke, as I stretch out my limbs and wrap them and my torso in the sacred smoke. As I do this, I pass the smudge pot from hand to hand. I've kind of got a rhythm that I use. It sets the tone for my day. When I'm finished, I put the smudge pot on a heatproof surface and scoop up the smoke in my hands as if I were washing my head in it. Then my area is smudged, I'm smudged, I'm in the right mindset, and I can start my day.

At times, you may be called to smudge other people, and this is fine as long as they are in agreement. I've done this at the start of ritual or as part of a healing. Use the smudge as I just described, making sure that their arms and legs (including their feet) as well as their torso and head have been touched by the sacred smoke. It's up to the other person how involved they want to be with the smudge. I've known people who have chosen to bathe in it, while for others just lightly passing through it was enough.

Your fur-kids can be smudged too, but go easy on the smoke.... Smudge your pets when they need an extra boost of love or protection.

Your fur-kids can be smudged too, but go easy on the smoke. I once had a dog who panicked at the smell of smoke, so if you see your animal showing any sign of distress, stop the process immediately. Smudge your pets when they need an extra boost of love or protection. The cleansing energy of the smudge coupled with your good intentions—when used properly—can only be a positive thing.

An Earth Day Smudge to Use Every Day

This smudge ceremony was started several years ago as an Earth Day observation, and was so well received that I have repeated it often whenever things feel a bit out of whack. It's similar to smudging yourself or an area, but in this case you're offering up your smoke for the Earth and all her children and her future.

You've probably heard the sayings "As above, so below," and "The microcosm is the macrocosm." You have a subtle body, which is the atmosphere around you, your different layers of energy. The Earth also has a subtle body around it, an atmosphere made up of layers. You might even have studied them when you were in school: the troposphere, stratosphere, mesosphere, thermosphere, and exosphere. Now, realistically, the smoke from the smudge is going to dissipate before it reaches the upper levels of the atmosphere. However, there is no limit to what the power of positive thinking can achieve.

Your Earth ceremony can be done alone or with others. Light your smudge as you normally do, and enter into a state of mindfulness about what you wish to achieve. Envision the planet growing smaller and smaller and smaller and the smoke from your herbs growing bigger and bigger and bigger until the whole planet is enveloped in the sacred smoke of your smudge. Let the smoke rise, and in your mind's eye, watch it permeate all the layers of the Earth's atmosphere with its cleansing and healing properties.

As the smoke starts to diminish, allow your mind to see the planet getting bigger and bigger while you and your smoke get smaller and smaller. Once the smudge is spent and any residue has cooled, empty your smudge pot onto the ground in a spot that has special meaning for you. (We have an orchard, and I usually put mine out there.) You may not have brought the world into balance—that would be a huge undertaking—but you've shown it some love and appreciation, and that always goes a long way toward cultivating harmony and wholeness.

The Smudging Herbs

Now that you know what smudge is and what to do with it, what herbs should you use? There's no hard-and-fast rule about this, and in my own practice, I have many herbs that I combine in various proportions to make different blends for different purposes. Remember, a good smudge depends on three things: the plant's magical properties, the way it smells when it burns, and its combustibility.

SAGE

This is my go-to herb. It is the anchor for everything I do, and there are some mornings when this is the only herb I use when I smudge. It is cleansing, purifying, and protective. Its smell is sweet and smoky, and it smolders well and produces a thick and pleasant smoke.

CEDAR

This was another one of the first herbs I used when I started to smudge. The dryad of the cedar tree is revered by many cultures. Cedar is protective, preserving, and purifying, and it smells warm and soothing.

LAVENDER

Do you remember the lavender sachets that were kept in dresser drawers? In addition to being sweet-smelling, lavender is another herb that protects and preserves. Its scent promotes peace of mind and relaxation.

CLOVES

This is a smell that people seem to either love or loathe—and I love it, particularly during the time between Samhain and Imbolc. It's warm and inviting and conjures up childhood memories for me. When added to a smudge blend, it offers a spicy scent and lots of uplifting energy.

Rosemary

Rosemary is one of the herbs immortalized in the song "Scarborough Fair," made famous in the 1960s by Simon and Garfunkel, but it actually dates back to the Middle Ages. It's both a medicinal herb and a culinary one. My husband even uses it in his traditional home-brewed ales. I use it in smudge blends that involve honor and remembrance.

. . . .

All living things have their own subtle body and their own energy signature—their own medicine. In his book *The Hero with a Thousand Faces*, Joseph Campbell introduces the idea that we are all the hero of our own odyssey, the adventure being this amazing journey called life. Every action contributes to the legacy that is being created. Even science agrees that for every action there is an equal and opposite reaction (Newton's third law of motion). Study the stories of your own culture and examine the popular mythological tales, and you will see things that you can relate to—after all, that is what makes a good story! Embracing good medicine teaches you to find the courage to be the hero of your own life, to create your destiny by being the changes you want to see unfold. Smudge blends—carefully chosen and used with mindfulness—are a wonderful way of using the energy of herbal essences to enhance your own journey through life.

Notes

Campbell, Joseph. *The Hero with a Thousand Faces.* 1949. Reprint, Princeton, NJ: Princeton University Press, 1973.

Kondo, Marie. *Tidying Up with Marie Kondo.* https://shop.konmari.com/pages/netflix.

Nautiyal, Chandra Shekhar, Puneet Singh Chauhan, and Yeshwant Laxman Nene. "Medicinal Smoke Reduces Airborne Bacteria." *Journal of Ethnopharmacology* 114, no. 3 (December 3, 2007): 446–451. www.sciencedirect .com/science/article/pii/S0378874107004357?via=ihub.

Charlie Rainbow Wolf *is happiest when she's creating something, especially if it's made from items that others have discarded. Pottery, writing, knitting, astrology, and tarot ignite her passion, but she happily confesses she's easily distracted—life offers such wonderful things to explore! A recorded singer-songwriter and published author, she champions holistic living and lives in the Midwest with her husband and special-needs Great Danes. Astrology reports, smudge pots, smudge blends, and more are available through her website at www.charlierainbow.com.*

Illustrator: Rik Olson

Give Your Life a Magical Boost with Oracle Cards

Deborah Blake

Many Witches use tarot cards, both for fun and for serious guidance. Some people even have large collections of cards tucked away in drawers or out on their altars. But it may not have occurred to you to add oracle cards to your magical toolkit. If that's true, it may be time to start a whole new obsession…I mean, collection.

The term *oracle card* can cover a pretty wide range of styles and approaches. In my own collection I have four different goddess-themed decks and a variety of others with affirmations, blessings, and, of course, Witches.

The great thing about oracle decks is that they are much easier to use than the tarot. I've been reading tarot professionally for over twenty years, and there are still times when something simpler is exactly what I need. You can use oracle cards for divination (as you would the tarot), general guidance, or magical work, or to get a suggestion for the appropriate action at the time of the reading.

Much like tarot decks, oracle decks come in many different sizes and shapes, and you may need to look at a few before you find the one that suits your needs. Or, like me, you may wish to own an assortment, so that you have a deck that is perfect for any occasion. Many of them have absolutely fabulous illustrations, so you may choose a deck as much for how it looks as for how it is used.

Goddess Oracle Deck Exploration

For instance, I have four different goddess decks. Kris Waldherr's *Goddess Inspiration Oracle* (Llewellyn) has eighty cards, each featuring a portrait of a goddess or manifestation of the divine feminine, along with a brief description of her attributes. Unlike in some decks, many of these goddesses are obscure, or at the very least are not commonly used in general Witchcraft, so they are great for expanding your practice and your knowledge. Each card has an inspirational statement, so they are helpful when you need a boost. For instance, the card featuring Psyche says, "Allow love to transform your soul. You are ready for it."

Another great goddess deck is *Goddesses Knowledge Cards* (Pomegranate) by artist Susan Seddon Boulet and writer Michael Babcock. This one has forty-eight cards, each of them featuring a goddess and a more detailed description. I also have *Journey to the Goddess Realm* (U.S. Games Systems) by Lisa Porter, which is along the same lines.

You can use these kinds of oracle decks to enhance your knowledge of goddesses, especially those you might not come across otherwise. You can also use them to open yourself to communication from a particular

goddess (it is always good to open doors) or to see if the goddesses have a message for you. My group, Blue Moon Circle, uses these goddess oracle cards during ritual from time to time for all of these purposes. For instance, we might pull a card from a goddess oracle on Imbolc to see which goddess we should be focusing on in the coming year.

I especially like to explore the goddess oracle decks in the quiet, more introspective months of winter. This seems to me like the perfect time to look inward and see which deities might be reflected there, as well as spend time in spiritual exploration and experimentation. If you do lunar magic, the night of a full moon is also a wonderful time to use oracle cards, especially those featuring goddesses.

Try this using any oracle deck that is goddess-centered. After the moon rises on the night of a full moon, find a quiet place where you can sit for a while undisturbed. If you have an outside area where you can actually sit under the moon, that's ideal, but realistically that isn't possible for everyone. If you can't be outside, you may want to take a moment before you start to gaze at the moon from wherever you are.

Then light a candle, waft yourself and your oracle deck with a sage wand if you want to, and ask the goddess to guide you to who or what you need to know. Spread the cards out upside down on a table or cloth in front of you. Let your dominant hand move slowly back and forth over the top of the cards until you feel one "pull" at you, or if that doesn't happen, just pick one randomly.

If there is a message on the card (or in the book that comes with the deck, if there is one), read it and see if there is something about it that resonates with your current situation. Look at the goddess on the card. Is she familiar to you? If she isn't, you may want to look into her mythology more deeply later on. Does she have attributes that you need or want? Spend some time connecting with the goddess and her message, then say thank you for the gift of her presence and snuff out the candle.

Other Oracle Approaches

Goddess oracle cards are only one approach, of course. There are many oracle decks that focus on even simpler affirmations or blessings. For instance, the *Conscious Spirit Oracle Deck* (U.S. Games Systems) by Kim Dreyer has forty-four cards and an accompanying guidebook that focus on "awakening the spirit and rekindling the connection between the cosmos and the earth." Each card has a title, like "Spark of the Divine" or "Air Elemental," and an affirmation. For instance, the Spark of the Divine card says, "I reignite the Divine spark within me and recognize I am part of all Creation."

This kind of deck is perfect for Witches who are actively working on reconnecting with nature, the divine, and their own innate power. That's most of us, I think! Two other decks that can help us connect with the essence of our Witchcraft path and aid our practice are the *Peace Oracle: Guidance for Challenging Times* (Blue Angel) by Toni Carmine Salerno and Leela J. Williams and *Blessed Be: Mystical Celtic Blessing Cards to Enrich & Empower* (Blue Angel) by Lucy Cavendish and one of my favorite witchy artists, June Starr Weils.

The *Peace Oracle* features simple messages such has "Abundance" or "Priority," along with a book that gives you a divinatory meaning and an affirmation for each card. This is perfect for someone who wants something as straightforward and uncomplicated as possible, but these kinds of cards can also be used in magical work by placing them on your altar to reinforce any spellwork you're doing and to serve as a visual focus.

The *Blessed Be* cards, as the title would suggest, are all blessings of one kind or another. For example, there is "A Blessing on a Friendship," which comes with an accompanying blessing in the guidebook. Each of these cards ends with "Blessed be." These cards can be used randomly to remind you of various blessings in your life but might be best utilized when you need a boost for some specific activity or intent.

I would be remiss, of course, if I didn't mention my favorite deck, the *Everyday Witch Oracle* (Llewellyn) by, um, me. Yes, I love oracle decks so much that I wrote the guidebook for one! The amazing illustrations were done by Elisabeth Alba, who also did the *Everyday Witch Tarot*. Nobody wants a set of cards with illustrations by me, I assure you.

What I love about these cards, besides how much fun they were to work on, is the opportunity they gave me to design the deck I hoped would be perfect for any need. This deck is made up of forty cards, plus an accompanying book, and the Witches pictured in it come in many different shapes, colors, and styles, just like real-life Witches. The cards are broken up into four sets of ten, each associated with a different element—Earth, Air, Fire, and Water. So the Earth cards include things like "Connect with Gaia" and "Prosperity and Abundance." Each suit has an affirmation card, a magic card, and a meditation card, among others.

In the book, there are suggestions for three different approaches for each card: action, divination, and magic. So you can either start out with your intention set ("Today I am looking for guidance on a concrete action to take") or pull a card and see which of the three options seems most appealing at the time ("Gee, I think that meditation would help me"). Or, of course, you can just pull a card and see what it says to you.

Simple Ways to Use Oracle Decks

There are numerous ways to use any of these oracle decks, or one of the hundreds of other options out there. For instance, you can do a simple one-card pull. This can be done either by shuffling the deck and pulling a card out at random, or spreading them out and running your hand over the top of them all, as I described earlier. Or, if you want to really delve into a deck, you can pull one card every day and go through the entire oracle.

With your one-card pull, there are still many different approaches you can take. Here are a few suggestions.

Guidance: To get a basic idea of what you need to be looking at in your life or a message that you need to receive, pull out one card at random.

Inspiration: If you need a card to use as a focus for magical work or to place on your altar as a reminder of what you need to be working on, you can look through the deck and pick out whichever one has the image or symbols or message you need at the moment.

Exploration: To explore a specific deck or push yourself to work on a deeper spiritual level, pull one card every day. You can either do this in the order the deck arrives in or shuffle the cards and see what shows up each day. This is also a good way to use a goddess deck and become acquainted with new-to-you goddesses, especially ones from cultures you might not be familiar with.

Fun: Pull a card whenever you want, just for the heck of it. If you don't have a specific goal, this is as good of an approach to oracle cards as any.

Divination: Of course, this is the typical use of tarot cards, but oracle cards can be used for divination as well. Try writing down your question, then pull a card at random to see if you can get an answer.

Magical Work: Many oracle decks can be used as an adjunct or a springboard to magical work. You can pull a card and let it inspire your magical path for the day, or go through the deck and find one that you think will be particularly helpful for whatever magical work you already have planned. Oracle cards can also be used during ritual, either solitary or group. Virtually all of the applications listed here can be used during a group ritual as well as by the individual Witch.

Although it is most typical to use oracle cards singly, you can also do some simple spreads, just as you would with a tarot deck. For instance, two cards could be used as past and present, or today and tomorrow. Three cards could be past, present, and future, or even messages from Maiden, Mother, and Crone. You can also take two or three random cards and see if the messages or images on them seem to combine in a meaningful way.

There is no wrong way to use oracle cards, just as there is no one "right" or perfect deck. As with everything else in Witchcraft, you just need to explore the options until you find the approach and the deck that works best for you—or, if you're anything like me, the ten decks. Either way, I hope you find the oracle cards that empower your magic and your spirit.

Deborah Blake *is the award-winning author of twelve books on modern Witchcraft, including* The Little Book of Cat Magic, The Goddess Is in the Details, Everyday Witchcraft, *and numerous other books from Llewellyn, along with the* Everyday Witch *tarot and oracle decks. She has published many articles in Llewellyn annuals, and her ongoing column,* "Everyday Witchcraft," *is featured in* Witches & Pagans *magazine.*

She has also written the Baba Yaga and Broken Rider paranormal romance series and the Veiled Magic urban fantasies from Berkley.

When not writing, Deborah runs the Artisans' Guild, a cooperative shop she founded with a friend in 1999, and also works as a jewelry maker, tarot reader, and energy healer. She lives in a 130-year-old farmhouse in rural upstate New York with multiple cats who supervise all her activities, both magical and mundane. She can be found at www.deborahblakeauthor.com.

Illustrator: M. Kathryn Thompson

Do the Magic,
Then Do the Work

Tess Whitehurst

Once you cast a spell, chances are good you're in for a positive change. But real magic is not like in the movies. In almost every case, your heart's desire will not suddenly materialize in a puff of smoke. It *will* materialize, but first you will be required to step up and do some work.

This is a good thing! Once you've set your eyes on the prize by casting your spell, you will often discover that the path toward the prize is more enriching than the prize itself. This is what makes magic a dynamic spiritual path and not just a quirky hobby.

To illustrate, consider that on the physical level, using magic to manifest a new car can be a wonderful thing. A new car will be a fun, safe, and reliable thing to have. But an even more valuable prize will be the personal evolution you experience in the process of manifesting your new car. Once your magic starts to work, you'll shift into believing that you deserve a new car, and you'll begin trusting the universe to provide for you more than you've ever trusted before. This, in turn, will open you up to even more abundance, happiness, and joy, not just in the short term but also for the rest of your life.

Here are some types of legwork you may feel guided or compelled to do once you have performed a spell for any purpose. When you familiarize yourself with these possibilities, you will be more alert to them when they arise. When you apply yourself to this work with enthusiasm and focus, you will manifest your intentions more quickly and with greater ease. And the benefits you'll reap in the process will be so much better than if your desire had instantly materialized in a boring old puff of smoke.

Using magic to manifest a new car can be a wonderful thing.... Once your magic starts to work, you'll shift into believing that you deserve a new car, and you'll begin trusting the universe to provide for you more than you've ever trusted before. This, in turn, will open you up to even more abundance, happiness, and joy.

Seek Opportunities

After you do a spell for a new job, what do you do the next day? Eat Belgian chocolate and binge-watch *Buffy the Vampire Slayer*? Nope! You actively look for a new job—*then* you eat chocolate and binge-watch *Buffy*. (After all, rest is important too, and chocolate is good for the soul!) Then, if necessary, you look for a new job again. And again. Until you find the job that's right for you.

The same is true regardless of your magical intention. Don't do a love spell and then sit at home waiting for your soul mate to knock on your door. Get out and have fun! Put yourself in situations where you will meet new people with similar interests. Or at the very least, download a dating app.

Clear Obstacles

Clearing clutter from your home, all on its own, is one of the most powerful acts of magic you can do. This is because clutter in your home (stuff you don't love, use, or need) represents stuck energy in your life and obstacles to your most ideal life momentum and flow. It follows that when you clear the clutter, it becomes exponentially easier to manifest the things you want. The same is true of digital clutter (old emails and downloads you no longer need) as well as clutter in your car, workspace, yard, wallet, purse, or storage areas.

That's why, after you do a spell, you may feel compelled to clear clutter out of your life: this will create a vacuum into which your intended blessings will irresistibly be drawn.

But clutter isn't the only type of obstacle you may feel the urge to clear. There are countless possibilities, but here's just one example. Let's say you do a spell to find a new apartment, and you have an obstacle to doing so in the form of a low credit score. In this case, you may "happen" to see a notice for a free class at your local library on raising your credit score, or *Credit Repair Kit for Beginners* may catch your eye at a used bookstore. You might even wake up one morning and think, "Hey, I bet I can figure out how to fix my credit score."

Cultivate Receptivity

In almost every case, if you want your spell to work, you need to be in a receptive state. This is because everything is energy, and when you cast a spell, you are consciously working with the energy of the universe in order to magnetize your heart's desire. If you're not receptive and open, you're not magnetic, and the object of your desire will have a hard time finding its way into your life.

How do you know if you're in a receptive state? Here are three helpful diagnostic indicators.

First, are you relaxed? It's natural if you're tense sometimes, but it's also important to tune into your body regularly to let go of any tension in your mind, muscles, and internal organs.

Second, how is your breathing? If it's shallow or ragged, smooth it out, deepen it, and slow it down. Do this regularly throughout the day.

And third, when people offer to help you, do you accept that help, at least some of the time? If your knee-jerk reaction is to turn down offers of assistance (whether they're from friends, family members, acquaintances, or total strangers), that's a good indicator that you're not in a receptive state. If you don't let other people help you, you're probably not going to let the universe help you either. In this case, set the intention to change this habit. The next time someone offers you assistance, ask yourself if you would actually benefit from the help they are offering. If the answer is yes, move out of your comfort zone by gracefully accepting that assistance. Over time, it will become easier and more natural to accept help. In turn, your magical intentions will manifest more reliably.

Listen to Your Intuition

In order to help your magical intention manifest in the quickest and most ideal way, cultivate an exquisitely sensitive awareness of your intuitive hits. Often, your intuition will alert you to a beneficial opportunity by filling you with a sense of adventure, possibility, or fun. Let's say you do a healing spell and then find yourself feeling weirdly enthusiastic about going to a different grocery store than you usually do. While shopping at the alternative store, perhaps you come across someone giving away free samples of an herbal remedy you hadn't considered before, which could be just the thing you need to help you heal.

Upgrade Your Beliefs

Some people hold the belief that they have excellent parking karma and always find the best parking spots. Other people go into a parking lot feeling pretty sure it's going to be a hassle to find a spot at all, let alone a good one. For both types of people, what they believe is absolutely true for them. This is because our beliefs and expectations contribute to our vibration, which in turn creates our experience. This is one of the core tenets of magic, and is one of the main dynamics that contributes to the effectiveness of spells.

Our beliefs and expectations contribute to our vibration, which in turn creates our experience. This is one of the core tenets of magic, and is one of the main dynamics that contributes to the effectiveness of spells.

This is why, once you perform a spell, you may find yourself being called to change your beliefs about yourself and your life. If you do a spell to create more time in your schedule so you don't feel rushed and stressed all the time, it's likely you will feel guided to look at your beliefs about time. Once you do, you might discover that you've been believing things like, "Only irresponsible people have extra time in their schedule to spend on themselves," or "You can't make good money unless you work more than forty hours a week."

Once you honestly assess the limiting beliefs you've been holding, you can shift them. First, you can question whether they're actually true, and remind yourself that there's no way for you to know definitively that they are true in all cases. Then you can look for proof that they are *not* true. Then you can write new beliefs that will serve you better and define your reality in a more desirable way. Using the previous example, your new beliefs could be, "It is a responsible act to take time for myself," and "Many people make plenty of money while working thirty hours a week or less."

Put in Time and Effort

Once, when I was still very new to the magical path, I did a money spell. Then I found a job waiting tables. Then I found another job waiting tables. Once I got the hang of each new job, I felt exhilarated by it, and when another server was looking for someone to cover their shift, I happily volunteered whenever I could. The spell inspired me to get enthusiastic about working hard, and in turn, the money started to pour in. While waiting tables is a far cry from a stack of hundred dollar bills appearing in a puff of smoke, it definitely did the trick.

The same is true for other magical intentions. Whether you've cast a spell for success, romance, healing, or anything else, taking positive action as you feel guided will always bring you closer to your goal.

. . . .

I'll admit it: when I first started working magic, I sort of hoped my desire *would* instantly materialize in a puff of smoke. Now that I understand how magic actually works, I much prefer the reality. When you do the magic and then follow through by doing the work, the benefits you reap will surprise and delight you, and improve your life experience for years and decades to come.

Tess Whitehurst *is a cohost of the* Magic Monday Podcast *as well as the founder and facilitator of the Good Vibe Tribe Online School of Magical Arts. She has written nine books that have been translated into eighteen languages, including* Unicorn Magic: Awaken to Mystical Energy & Embrace Your Personal Power. *She's also the author of the* Magic of Flowers Oracle *and the* Cosmic Dancer Oracle. *She lives in the Rocky Mountains of Colorado. Visit her at tesswhitehurst.com.*

Illustrator: Bri Hermanson

Using Animal Energy &
Body Parts in Magickal Work
Raven Digitalis

When we think about classic witchy imagery and depictions of witchcraft, the use of herbs and animal parts may come to mind. Despite the prejudice of misinformed folks who think we sacrifice black cats (it was actually the Christian Church who murdered tens of thousands of cats as "Witches' familiars" in the Middle Ages), as well as the accusations of animal sacrifice (which is not as black-and-white a subject as it may seem), the truth is we Neopagan Witches have a deep respect for Mother Nature and her creatures great and small.

There's something about animals that speaks to the heart of the Witch—and to any genuine spiritual seeker. Like children, animals embody a type of innocence, an effortless connection to the ebbs and flows of life. We can learn a lot about living—and dying—from our animal comrades.

Perspectives of Consciousness

Speaking of animals, humans are a strange variety, to be sure. Although we are clearly "animal," there's something different about our consciousness, our evolutionarily advancements. It's something that science can't quite explain but can only theorize about. Why are we so different from other animals? Are we half-alien? Who knows!

Although ancient Western culture and some Asian cultures have a philosophical history of perceiving a *massive* divide between the animal and human realms, we know at this point that we ourselves are biological animals and that all animals are conscious beings: we all have a soul, feelings, intelligence, and purpose.

The glory and wonder of the animal kingdom is not something I feel the need to explain or persuade readers about. The name of this almanac is the *Witches' Companion*, after all, which tells me that you, as a reader, have a veneration and respect for the natural world—and probably have felt this from an early age! Witches and other sensitive mystics tend to carry a noticeable amount of empathy and compassion toward "the other," whoever or whatever that may be.

Pets and Familiars

What a miracle and blessing animals are in our lives! At the time of this writing, I have just finished having a very cozy and refreshing snuggle session with one of my three black cats, Fizzgig. A unique Maine Coon, Fizzy was born with seven kinks in her little poof-tail.

Sometimes my Priestess and I will gently grab it and cackle, "C'mere! Gimme dat tail for a spell!"

We nature workers feel an emotional bond with our pets. For all intents and purposes, and casting aside any nonsense from the past, pets are our familiars. Pets are our dear friends and are truly part of the family.

The whole concept of Witches having "familiars" is rooted in medieval European superstition. The term comes from the Latin *famulus*, "servant." Familiars were believed to be shapeshifting demons, faeries, and supernatural creatures who would at times assume the guise of animals (including pets) and whose role it was to assist the Witch in their deviant, heretical spellcasting. Naturally, this wild concept led to the torture and execution of countless innocent animals alongside their innocent owners.

Most Witches I know have ethical issues with using their pet's "bits" in spells, and this is perfectly understandable. I feel the same way. Although I am apt to carry a little bag of brushed-off kitty fluff during traveling adventures—in order to maintain a strong energetic connection to my cats—there's no way I would use their fur or whiskers in a spell, aside from making a simple offering to the goddess Bastet (Bast) or perhaps using the fur of one of my friend's dogs as an offering to Hekate. Still, every Witch is different and every magickal scenario is different.

Each species of animal has a different level of consciousness, a different vibration. Each relates differently to one another and to humans. For some reason, it feels wrong to me to use the parts of a pet cat or dog in a spell, unless it is designed to heal that pet, or to connect with the oversoul (greater consciousness) of Feline or Canine, for example. But other types of animals, such as a pet snake or tarantula, carry a different vibratory level of consciousness as it relates to humankind; I wouldn't think twice about utilizing their sheds for banishing work. Similarly,

I will use feathers from my chickens in magickal workings without worrying about who the feather came from, because they are not really "pets" to me (despite the fact that they live lavishly!). Again, the emotional relationship between animal and owner carries a significant metaphysical weight. In the end, it comes down to the Witch's personal intuition and ethics.

Whereas most Witches refer to their pets as their *familiars*, it should be known that some Witches do work with *familiar spirits*, which is to say, nonphysical spiritual helpers. This subject can be explored in depth in the fascinating book *The Witch's Familiar* written by my dearly departed friend Raven Grimassi.

Oversouls and Nonphysical Animals

One of the coolest things I learned early in my teenage Wiccan training was the concept of the animal *oversoul*. This is the belief that not only does any particular animal have an individual consciousness and personality, but there also exists a *collective consciousness* of any given animal (or plant, tree, etc.). The same can be said for us humans, no doubt!

When working with animal parts in magickal work, it is wise to call upon the oversoul of any given animal. Think of it as calling upon the Great God or the Great Goddess rather than a specific god or goddess.

The oversoul, or collective consciousness, of Snake, for example, embodies all the serpentine characteristics and their metaphysical attributes. Many believe that *sub-oversouls* exist, in that a python or a rattlesnake has a different collective consciousness than Snake as a whole but is obviously intricately related.

I appreciate the fact that we don't *need* to have a part of any given animal to call upon its oversoul. The mind and emotions are intricately tied to—even inseparable from—magick and spirituality. If we can tap into the essence of an animal by means of deep meditation alone, awesome! Most people, though, prefer to use some sort of imagery. If it isn't

an actual "piece" of that physical animal, it's a sketch or photographic image. Focus the mind, and the magickal energy naturally follows.

A *spirit animal* refers to a person's animal guide on the astral plane, and it is believed that everyone has one or more spirit animals at any given point in their life. Some people feel as though their spirit animal is an individual being, even giving it a name (or intuiting its name), which is more closely linked to the concept of a nonphysical familiar spirit. Most people who observe their spirit animal(s) view it more as an oversoul. For example, I work with the Great Raven and the Great Raven works with me, although I have never perceived an individual astral raven as a guide.

> **A *spirit animal* refers to a person's animal guide on the astral plane, and it is believed that everyone has one or more spirit animals at any given point in their life.**

A *power animal*, on the other hand, is a term given to a spiritual animal who appears for a short period of time in order to lend its medicine to a practitioner. For example, I went through a period of constantly seeing mules and donkeys, so I chose to heavily research their spiritual energy and to communicate with their oversouls to learn the lessons being delivered. The term *power animal* may also be applied to the oversoul of an animal that a person calls upon and consciously chooses to work with for one reason or another.

These terms should not be confused with a *totem animal*, which refers to the guardians of a particular tribe, clan, or family and/or an area of land. This concept is recognized in indigenous cultures across the globe, and should be respected as a deeply ingrained cultural and spiritual tradition. Practices of totemism, animal magick, and shapeshifting in a Neopagan context can be explored in the brilliant work of Lupa. (See the "Resources & Further Reading" section at the end of this article.)

Animal Life, Animal Death

If a Witch or earth-based magician is working directly with animal parts, there are some very important things to take into consideration.

Although the oversoul of any given animal species is easily accessible and workable, what about the individual animal itself whose body part is being utilized?

Humans have a profoundly larger sense of "self," or ego, than other animal species. Regardless, we all understand that animals are conscious beings who have their own sense of self-awareness and "I"-dentity. For this reason, we must be considerate of the source from which any given animal part is obtained. In the case of snakeskin, antler sheds, a feather, poop, or something similar found in nature, it's unlikely that any sort of pain was experienced by the animal when the item was shed. Because these items have been cast off, there aren't too many karmic considerations to worry about. Cruelty-free is the way to go!

If we know how the animal lived and died, we may feel ethically and karmically justified to utilize its bits. If, as is common in practices like hoodoo, we do not know the origin of the animal from which the part was cultivated, we enter something of a gray area.

When it comes to working with animals on a daily basis, namely dietarily, we must remember that not all meat is created equal. We as earth-based practitioners absolutely *must* research the reality of slaughterhouses and come into full awareness of the horrific abuse of factory "farming" as compared to humane, small-scale methods of raising animals for their "parts," such as meat, eggs, and dairy. In my belief, in an ideal world, *all Pagans and earth-based practitioners* would either choose a vegetarian diet or choose to strictly consume meat that is humanely sourced. Period. End of story.

Many food corporations are *finally* seeing the value of treating animals humanely. Even some major corporations, like Wendy's, source their beef from local farm suppliers instead of industrial farms, working with humane standards.

So how about us as Witches? What is our position on animal rights? Here's my take: *Animals are embodiments of nature through consciousness.* As people who worship and work with Mother Nature and her cycles, we have both the requirement and the responsibility to promote the protection, health, and wellness of nature in all her forms. If we're not recycling, eating humanely, and supporting Earth-loving companies, what kind of Pagans are we?

Crafty Components

Different practitioners utilize animal parts in different ways. We might see a shamanic practitioner wearing a necklace of bones, or a hoodoo practitioner carrying a badger's tooth for luck. The spiritual usage of animal parts is vast, and spans centuries of metaphysical practice.

Because we live in an age of instant communication, where knowledge is literally at our fingertips (hello, smartphone), we must have personal accountability in respecting the customs of cultures foreign to our own. We may take hints from some of their methods or even become formally trained in a tradition, but part of modern Witchcraft is utilizing our discernment to know when and when not to adopt or adapt a cultural practice.

Keep in mind that if you use an animal part for any act of magick, it must feel right. If something feels "off" about it, listen to your intuition. I once tried to use an alligator foot in a spell, but I continually felt a sensation of anger, or a lack of consent, coming from the item. My guess is that the alligator itself may not have been raised or killed in an ethical manner, so as a show of respect, I decided to craft the spell using only herbal parts instead of burying the alligator's paw in the earth.

Here is a list of various animal parts a person might choose to utilize in ritual, along with some suggested uses. The way you choose to utilize the parts depends entirely on the magick you are working, the medicine of the animal's oversoul, and the historical uses of any given animal part across global traditions.

ANTLERS

Antlers represent the masculine aspect and the energy of combat (including setting boundaries) and are emblematic of the Horned God seen across so many cultures.

Suggested Uses: Affix antlers above a home doorway for protection; place antlers on any nature god altar or shrine; craft antlers into a headpiece to connect with the masculine current during solar rituals.

BIRD FEET

A common hoodoo component, bird feet are believed to provide protection, as they are capable of "scratching" and dispersing energy.

Suggested Uses: Use a bird foot in magick to "scratch away" something that represents that which should be banished; hang bird feet outside the home to ward off unwanted influences.

BONES AND SKULLS

In numerous indigenous cultures and modern traditions based on ancient practices, we see that bones are one of the most commonly used items for divination (alongside shells). Bones carry the deepest energetic essence of any given animal.

Suggested Uses: Place bones or skulls on altars devoted to gods of nature; hang or place bones on an elemental shrine to the water element in the west (the direction in which we see the sun set or "die" each day); create art using bones to honor a particular animal; meditate with bones to connect with that animal's oversoul.

Claws

Like feet, the claws of an animal represent protection from harm and carry principles based on the animal from which they come.

Suggested Uses: Place one or more claws in a spell bag for protection; carry one in each pocket to boost energetic protection in daily life.

Dairy

Dairy items (including milk, eggs, and butter) are attuned to the Great Goddess energy because only biological females produce them. Their spiritual uses range all the way from offering ghee (clarified butter) and sacred milk in Hinduism to the hoodoo practice of rubbing an egg on the body to remove evils.

Suggested Uses: Pour milk on murtis (statues) of Hindu gods you wish to honor; rub an egg on the body to remove evils (then smash it); enchant butter under the light of the full moon to carry Goddess blessings forward when you eat it.

Feathers and Wings

Feathers and wings represent freedom and spiritual flight and are used in esoteric manners wherever birds are found, which is everywhere!

Suggested Uses: Create art using feathers and wings to represent personal freedom; rub a black feather on the body to remove external negativity (then burn it); use a wing or feather to waft the smoke from incense and sage around a person or within a home to aid in energetic cleansing.

Fossils

Fossils, such as the so-called dragon bones and teeth sold by some occult shops, represent the earth's deepest history and hidden knowledge.

Suggested Uses: Meditate with fossils to connect to ancient earth energy and receive visions of past lives; put a fossil in the bathtub with you to invoke the earth's primordial energy; incorporate a small fossil into magickal work aimed at personal evolution and deepening internal wisdom.

FUR AND PELTS

These animal parts depend on the magick of the animal from which they come. Please be exceedingly careful in ethically sourcing fur.

Suggested Uses: Craft pelts into medicine bags designed for healing; use a small pelt to wrap tools of divination; blow a tuft of fur into a wind to make a wish.

INSECTS

Like other animals, each insect carries a different vibrational medicine. The spider and the fly are very different creatures! As with all magickal work utilizing animal parts, do sufficient research and reflection on the animal's medicine. Please don't kill any bugs for magickal use.

Suggested Uses: Place insect corpses in a banishing bag designed to be cremated (such as a sachet or poppet used at Samhain); offer a dead bug at the base of a live plant or tree (death feeding life); write "I release _____" on a piece of paper, put a dead bug on it, crumple the paper, then throw it in the trash.

NESTS

Naturally, nests represent the house and home, symbolizing domestic protection and cooperation.

Suggested Uses: Nail a nest above a door (home or bedroom) to symbolize protection and safety; place your magickal keepsakes inside a nest that you've found in order to keep their energies protected.

Poop

Across the board, animal droppings represent banishing and casting away unwanted energies that have already been processed or "digested" in life.

Suggested Uses: Bury an animal's feces in the earth while saying a self-made chant designed to release unwanted energies or influences; place an animal's dried poop in a cloth bag to connect with the essence of that animal whenever you choose, such as while meditating, working, or traveling.

Regurgitations

Regurgitated materials, including hairballs and owl pellets, are similar to poop but represent a more forceful banishing or rejection of energy.

Suggested Uses: Throw a regurgitation into flowing water or out the car window at a crossroads while visualizing those things you wish to forcefully cast away from your life.

Sheddings

Through and through, animal molts carry the energy of outgrowing the old and making way for the new.

Suggested Uses: Burn an animal molt while performing a ritual aimed at releasing old energies, mindsets, and emotional patterns that no longer serve you.

Shells

The shells of crustaceans, snails, and other invertebrates are emblems of protection from harm. The same can be said of exoskeletons and eggshells.

Suggested Uses: Use shells in the bathtub to connect with the ancient energy of Mother Ocean; place shells around the home to give it a boost of protection; make a barrier or circle of protection using pulverized eggshells.

Teeth

Used for processing food, teeth metaphysically vibrate with "chewing" life's experiences and gaining sustenance through effort. Fangs additionally represent protection and self-defense.

Suggested Uses: Keep an animal's teeth in a spell bag for protection or to connect with the animal's oversoul; make jewelry using teeth to keep that particular animal's energy near you at any given time.

The Human Animal

Witches, magicians, and esoteric folks of all stripes understand that we can utilize our own animal bits in prayer and magickal work. Any body part from any type of animal is sacred and potentially magickal. The same can be said about our own *human* bits and pieces.

Any body part from any type of animal is sacred and potentially magickal. The same can be said about our own *human* bits and pieces.

Some examples of bits we can use from ourselves include blood (including menstrual), dead skin, hair, fingernail or toenail clippings, tears, sexual fluids, feces, urine, vomit, and so on, with each "part" carrying a different interpretive meaning. Just keep in mind that a *direct* link to our very essence as a person, including our karma and experience of life, is contained in any part of ourselves that we utilize. We should be very wise when utilizing our own parts for magickal work. This direct link is not something to be taken lightly.

A direct and intense magickal link also occurs, of course, when we use *other people's* bits in magickal work. Naturally, this is a slippery slope.

If you choose to utilize human parts in ritual, it's best to work with your own (or none at all). Although it might seem cool and Gothy to have a human bone as a magick wand, that individual person must be taken into consideration. If we are working magick *at the behest of* another person, and they approve our use of hair in a healing ceremony, for example, that's entirely different, because it is solicited, approved, and ethical. It is best to utilize the parts of another person only if they give their express consent, such as for a healing spell.

As I mentioned earlier, humans have a unique cognitive and emotional processing ability, so there is a greater sense of "I" or "self" in the human animal. Our spirits are more prone to becoming attached to the physical plane, its inhabitants, and our own body vehicles. This is why so many humans become disembodied spirits (ghosts), while animals tend to move on to the next experience at a faster rate.

Just the same, when we utilize the parts of beloved animal allies, we have the spiritual responsibility to communicate with the animal's oversoul in order to approach their energy with the utmost respect and humility. This reverence for the natural world is the heart of the Craft.

Resources & Further Reading

Andrews, Ted. *Animal-Speak: The Spiritual & Magical Powers of Creatures Great & Small*. St. Paul, MN: Llewellyn, 1993.

Cunningham, Scott. *Cunningham's Encyclopedia of Magical Herbs*. St. Paul, MN: Llewellyn, 1984.

Digitalis, Raven. *Shadow Magick Compendium: Exploring Darker Aspects of Magickal Spirituality*. Woodbury, MN: Llewellyn, 2008.

Freuler, Kate. *Of Blood and Bones: Working with Shadow Magick & the Dark Moon*. Woodbury, MN: Llewellyn, 2019.

Farrar, Stewart, and Janet Farrar. *A Witches' Bible: The Complete Witches' Handbook*. Custer, WA: Phoenix Publishing, 1981.

Grandin, Temple. *Animals Make Us Human: Creating the Best Life for Animals.* New York: Mariner Books, 2010.

Grimassi, Raven. *The Witch's Familiar: Spiritual Partnership for Successful Magic.* St. Paul, MN: Llewellyn, 2003.

Lupa. *Fang and Fur, Blood and Bone: A Primal Guide to Animal Magic.* Stafford, UK: Megalithica Books, 2006.

———. *New Paths to Animal Totems: Three Alternative Approaches to Creating Your Own Totemism.* Woodbury, MN: Llewellyn, 2012.

McNevin, Estha. *Opus Aima Obscuræ.* Tradition materials and lesson notes. Missoula, MT, 2003–present.

Roderick, Timothy. *The Once Unknown Familiar: Shamanic Paths to Unleash Your Animal Powers.* St. Paul, MN: Llewellyn, 1994.

Silverknife, Zanoni. *Lessons in Georgian Wicca, 101–104.* Class handouts and lecture notes. Missoula, MT, 1999.

Yronwode, Catherine. *Hoodoo Herb and Root Magic: A Materia Magica of African-American Conjure.* Forestville, CA: Lucky Mojo Curio Co., 2002.

Raven Digitalis (*Missoula, MT*) *is the author of* The Everyday Empath, Esoteric Empathy, Shadow Magick Compendium, Planetary Spells & Rituals, *and* Goth Craft, *all from Llewellyn. He is the cofounder of a nonprofit multicultural temple called Opus Aima Obscuræ (OAO), which primarily observes Neopagan and Hindu traditions. Raven has been an earth-based practitioner since 1999, a Priest since 2003, a Freemason since 2012, and an empath all his life. He holds a degree in cultural anthropology from the University of Montana and is also a professional Tarot reader, DJ, card-carrying magician, small-scale farmer, and animal rights advocate. Visit him at:*

www.ravendigitalis.com
www.facebook.com/ravendigitalis
www.opusaimaobscurae.org
www.facebook.com/opusaimaobscurae

Illustrator: Tim Foley

A Witch's Practical Guide to Visiting Sacred Sites

Laura Tempest Zakroff

For a Witch, there is nothing quite like visiting a sacred site. Once you set foot on those grounds, you become part of history—connecting with not only the memories of the land itself but also the experiences of everyone who has come before you to that place. And I do mean everyone—from ancient residents to the tourists who stopped by an hour before you.

In the past couple of years, I've managed to check off some major sites that I've been pining to see for most of my life. While on tour across the United States, I gazed at the petroglyphs in southern Utah, lost myself in the spiral of the Serpent Mound in Ohio, and marveled at the mysteries of the cliff dwellers in Mesa Verde, Colorado. On a recent trip to England, I drank from both the Red and the White Spring in Glastonbury, laid my hands on practically every stone in Avebury, and stood inside the circle at Stonehenge at sunrise days before the solstice. There were also some special stops where the history is much more recent and the setting far more urban: teaching in the same room where Gerald Gardner's coven met in the basement at Atlantis Bookshop in London and visiting the apartment complex where Doreen Valiente once lived in Brighton.

Visiting these special places can provide amazing magical experiences that will inspire your practice and invigorate your spirit. However, these experiences can also be frustrating, exhausting, expensive, and even dangerous without proper planning. So I've collected some advice garnered from my own experiences that I hope will aid you on your own journeys.

Connecting with the Spirit of Place

No matter what kind of site it is, upon arrival, I always try to take a few moments to absorb the atmosphere. Be sure to survey the landscape, making note of plants and animals—or structures and people—that surround you. What does the air smell like? How does your body respond to the place? How does it make you feel, outside of your own emotions and thoughts? Read it as you would a friend's facial expressions and body language. Cataloging this information mentally can aid you in determining how you might best connect with the place.

Connecting with the spirit of place can be a very hands-on experience for me—literally. I will stop to gently place a palm on a nearby tree or stone, or kneel down and sink my hands into the grass. Often, if there's seating provided, it will offer not only a wonderful view but also an opportunity to situate yourself in the place. If "no touching" is the rule, well, there are still my feet to connect with the earth, my eyes to behold it, and my lungs to take it in.

Interacting with the Site

Every site is obviously going to be different, with its own rules and procedures. That means "be respectful" should be your baseline, and listen carefully to the instructions of the docents, volunteers, rangers, or staff.

Always consider your impact on a site, especially if it's situated in nature versus inside a building. I know folks who insist on leaving offerings and others who must take a memento with them. I understand the logic of both, and they can be appropriate in certain situations, but you can't apply that agenda to every site. Some places encourage you to participate in lighting a candle, making a mark, leaving a coin, ringing a bell, and so on. But other sites may be very delicate habitats, where the touching or moving of earth, stones, plants, etc., can be very harmful. Offerings of unapproved or non-native foods and other plants can wreak havoc on the local flora and fauna. Synthetic ribbons, metal, glitter and other non-biodegradable items can also cause lasting damage. At sites where you're supposed to make an offering, they generally provide the materials (for free or a small donation), so that's the best course of action. Because really, it's the intent that counts, not your ego. If you feel you must leave something behind as an offering, consider your breath. You can also make a small donation to help protect the site.

I feel the best approach is to leave no trace on a site, and in fact clean up when you see obvious litter. My partner and I have collected trash we found at less-regulated sites and properly disposed of it afterward. The site will appreciate your effort.

Sacred in the Eyes of the Beholder

Historically, we tend to think of pilgrimages in the context of traveling to religious sites—temples, churches, shrines, gravesites, etc. But from a more modern perspective, a sacred site can have historical, artistic, spiritual, personal, and others kinds of significance—depending on who you ask. The combination of significance and the cumulative act of visitation essentially defines a sacred site, meaning if it's important to someone and draws people to it, you have yourself a sacred site of some sort. Whether it's the Space Needle in Seattle, the Cathedral Basilica of Saint Louis in Missouri, Marie Laveau's tomb in New Orleans, or Carhenge in Nebraska, there's a certain magic to be found in these places. There is the power of the place itself, and then there is another level of energy created by the progression of visitors over time. The curiosity of the visitors, their witnessing the space, and their physical investment of time and money all build upon the site.

Remember that not everyone is visiting for the same reason, meaning not everyone has the same intent or perspective on a site that you may have. For some, it's a mandatory school trip, a family vacation, a research project, or a memorial to a loved one. How other people behave at a site is out of your hands. To avoid being annoyed or frustrated, focus on why you are there.

Do Your Research and Plan Ahead

If you have flexibility in your schedule and the opportunity to plan ahead, then by all means take advantage of it. When I'm on the road, I might not know if I can visit a site until the last minute, which can lead to a host of complications. Check the hours—and recheck them for the time of year you are visiting and any possible effects the weather or government tomfoolery may have on them. Some sites are staffed by volunteers, so while they may advertise as being open from 1:00 to 4:00 p.m., the volunteer may call in sick or show up two hours late. Or the website may say they are open from 9:00 a.m. to 5:00 p.m., but they stop letting people in at 4:00 p.m. Some special areas may require tickets—and during the busy season, they sell out fast, so you may want to reserve them in advance versus taking your chances, especially if you have a limited amount of time to visit.

What's the parking situation? Some sites are free if you access them by foot but you can only park in certain places that cost money—or are located in a reserve that requires an entry fee for vehicles. Consult the website or brochure about accessibility restrictions and potential health risks. Some sites require precarious descents or crawling through small spaces to access them, so there will be warnings about these to heed. If you're afraid of heights or claustrophobic, have a heart condition, or require assistance for mobility, the last thing you want to find out after driving six hours is that you won't be able to get to the site comfortably.

Know Yourself

If crowds are upsetting to you, then you definitely should do some research to see when the busy times are, such as weekends versus weekdays or days that are school vacations. Certain sites have free days, and while you may save some money, you will likely have to contend with a lot of people. You can also get up early to visit a site while everyone else is just waking and thinking about breakfast.

There's also the weather to consider. If you don't mind conditions that are less than ideal, you might end up with the whole place to yourself. For example, we visited Avebury on a Wednesday afternoon that was mostly cloudy and a bit windy. The rain held off until later in the day and the sun came out to visit off and on, so it was perfect weather but temperamental enough to turn other folks away. We barely ran into anyone else—it was fantastic!

Be Smart, Be Safe

Pay attention to signs and restrictions. I like to say that if there's a sign, there's a reason for it—usually inspired by the actions of a previous human. Don't be that person they have to airlift out of a ravine because you thought it would be just fine to step over the rope to take a quick selfie.

> **Pay attention to signs and restrictions. I like to say that if there's a sign, there's a reason for it... Don't be that person they have to airlift out of a ravine because you thought it would be just fine to step over the rope to take a quick selfie.**

Before you head out, charge your phone fully and download a map of the area in case there's no signal. Wear proper footwear. It may be hot in the desert, but closed-toe shoes are a lot safer than sandals if there is the possibility of stumbling across stinging insects and snakes. If the conditions are wet, pack extra socks, especially if you don't have waterproof shoes. Even trekking through dew-covered grass can make for miserable soggy feet very quickly. Bring a hat and apply sunscreen, even if it's cloudy or overcast. Bring water in a reusable bottle. If you're going to be doing a fair amount of hiking, then bring along a pocket knife, matches, tissues, some snacks, and some long sleeves. I also like to take a small notebook for recording my thoughts and making sketches. Pay attention to the weather report before you go out. Be realistic about your health and conscious of the environment—sites that are at higher altitudes can bring on elevation sickness pretty quickly.

Make the Time and Manifest It

If you truly want to visit a site, the best piece of advice I can give you is to start planning on it. If your thinking is, "I'll never have the time/money/opportunity to go there," then you're the one squashing your own dreams. Engage magical thinking—if you start to visualize your trip, you can make it happen. With some planning and ingenuity, you can definitely visit many places on a shoestring budget. If you're worried about accessibility, *do* contact the people maintaining the site and see what options can be made available.

Last but Not Least

You don't necessarily have to go far to experience the sacred and the special. You might be surprised at what's hanging out in your own back yard, just down the street in your own hometown, or in the next town over. You can find and connect with the sacred wherever you are.

Laura Tempest Zakroff *is a professional artist, author, performer, and Modern Traditional Witch residing in New England. She is the author of* Weave the Liminal, Sigil Witchery, The Witch's Cauldron, *and* The Witch's Altar *(with Jason Mankey), and she edited* The New Aradia: A Witch's Handbook to Magical Resistance. *Laura is the artist and author of the* Liminal Spirits Oracle, *blogs for Patheos as* A Modern Traditional Witch *and for Witches & Pagans as* Fine Art Witchery, *and contributes to* The Witches' Almanac, Ltd. *Visit her at www.LauraTempestZakroff.com.*

Illustrator: Rik Olson

The Lunar Calendar

September 2020 to December 2021

SEPTEMBER
S	M	T	W	T	F	S
		1	2	3	4	5
6	7	8	9	10	11	12
13	14	15	16	17	18	19
20	21	22	23	24	25	26
27	28	29	30			

OCTOBER
S	M	T	W	T	F	S
				1	2	3
4	5	6	7	8	9	10
11	12	13	14	15	16	17
18	19	20	21	22	23	24
25	26	27	28	29	30	31

NOVEMBER
S	M	T	W	T	F	S
1	2	3	4	5	6	7
8	9	10	11	12	13	14
15	16	17	18	19	20	21
22	23	24	25	26	27	28
29	30					

DECEMBER
S	M	T	W	T	F	S
		1	2	3	4	5
6	7	8	9	10	11	12
13	14	15	16	17	18	19
20	21	22	23	24	25	26
27	28	29	30	31		

2021

JANUARY
S	M	T	W	T	F	S
					1	2
3	4	5	6	7	8	9
10	11	12	13	14	15	16
17	18	19	20	21	22	23
24	25	26	27	28	29	30
31						

FEBRUARY
S	M	T	W	T	F	S
	1	2	3	4	5	6
7	8	9	10	11	12	13
14	15	16	17	18	19	20
21	22	23	24	25	26	27
28						

MARCH
S	M	T	W	T	F	S
	1	2	3	4	5	6
7	8	9	10	11	12	13
14	15	16	17	18	19	20
21	22	23	24	25	26	27
28	29	30	31			

APRIL
S	M	T	W	T	F	S
				1	2	3
4	5	6	7	8	9	10
11	12	13	14	15	16	17
18	19	20	21	22	23	24
25	26	27	28	29	30	

MAY
S	M	T	W	T	F	S
						1
2	3	4	5	6	7	8
9	10	11	12	13	14	15
16	17	18	19	20	21	22
23	24	25	26	27	28	29
30	31					

JUNE
S	M	T	W	T	F	S
		1	2	3	4	5
6	7	8	9	10	11	12
13	14	15	16	17	18	19
20	21	22	23	24	25	26
27	28	29	30			

JULY
S	M	T	W	T	F	S
				1	2	3
4	5	6	7	8	9	10
11	12	13	14	15	16	17
18	19	20	21	22	23	24
25	26	27	28	29	30	31

AUGUST
S	M	T	W	T	F	S
1	2	3	4	5	6	7
8	9	10	11	12	13	14
15	16	17	18	19	20	21
22	23	24	25	26	27	28
29	30	31				

SEPTEMBER
S	M	T	W	T	F	S
			1	2	3	4
5	6	7	8	9	10	11
12	13	14	15	16	17	18
19	20	21	22	23	24	25
26	27	28	29	30		

OCTOBER
S	M	T	W	T	F	S
					1	2
3	4	5	6	7	8	9
10	11	12	13	14	15	16
17	18	19	20	21	22	23
24	25	26	27	28	29	30
31						

NOVEMBER
S	M	T	W	T	F	S
	1	2	3	4	5	6
7	8	9	10	11	12	13
14	15	16	17	18	19	20
21	22	23	24	25	26	27
28	29	30				

DECEMBER
S	M	T	W	T	F	S
		1	2	3	4	
5	6	7	8	9	10	11
12	13	14	15	16	17	18
19	20	21	22	23	24	25
26	27	28	29	30	31	

SEPTEMBER 2020

SU	M	T	W
30	**31**	**1** 2nd ≈ ☽ v/c 12:56 am ☽ → ♓ 5:34 am	**1** 2nd ♓ Full Moon 1:22 am ○ *Harvest Moon*
6 3rd ♈ ☽ v/c 12:45 am ♀ → ♌ 3:22 am ☽ → ♉ 4:43 am	**7** 3rd ♉ *Labor Day*	**8** 3rd ♉ ☽ v/c 8:47 am ☽ → ♊ 5:28 pm	**9** 3rd ♊ ♂ ℞ 6:22 pm *Mars retrograde*
13 4th ♋ ☽ v/c 8:05 am ☽ → ♌ 11:32 am	**14** 4th ♌	**15** 4th ♌ ☽ v/c 11:09 am ☽ → ♍ 2:37 pm	**16** 4th ♍
20 1st ♏	**21** 1st ♏ ☽ v/c 2:13 pm ☽ → ♐ 3:32 pm	**22** 1st ♐ ☉ → ♎ 9:31 am *Mabon* *Sun enters Libra* *Fall Equinox*	**22** 1st ♐ ☽ v/c 1:31 pm ☽ → ♑ 7:16 pm 2nd Quarter 9:55 pm ◑
27 2nd ≈ ☿ → ♏ 3:41 am	**28** 2nd ≈ ☽ v/c 3:18 am ☽ → ♓ 11:34 am	**29** 2nd ♓ ♄ D 1:11 am	**30** 2nd ♓ ☽ v/c 1:30 pm ☽ → ♈ 10:47 pm
4	**5**	**6**	**7**

Eastern Daylight Time (EDT)

ZODIAC SIGNS

♈ Aries	♌ Leo	♐ Sagittarius
♉ Taurus	♍ Virgo	♑ Capricorn
♊ Gemini	♎ Libra	≈ Aquarius
♋ Cancer	♏ Scorpio	♓ Pisces

PLANETS

☉ Sun	♃ Jupiter
☽ Moon	♄ Saturn
☿ Mercury	♅ Uranus
♀ Venus	♆ Neptune
♂ Mars	♇ Pluto

SEPTEMBER 2020

TH	F	SA	NOTES
3 3rd ♓ ☽ v/c 10:34 am ☽ → ♈ 4:22 pm	**4** 3rd ♈	**5** ☿ → ♎ 3:46 pm	
10 3rd ♊ 4th Quarter 5:26 am ◑	**11** 4th ♊ ☽ v/c 12:48 am ☽ → ♋ 4:23 am	**12** 4th ♋ ♃ D 8:41 pm	
17 4th ♍ New Moon 7:00 am ● ☽ v/c 7:42 am ☽ → ♎ 2:56 pm *New Moon*	**18** 1st ♎	**19** 1st ♎ ☽ v/c 10:29 am ☽ → ♏ 2:33 pm	
24 2nd ♑	**25** 2nd ♑ ☽ v/c 11:36 pm	**26** 2nd ♑ ☽ → ♒ 2:08 am	
1	*2*	*3*	
8	*9*	*10*	

Aspects & Moon Phases

☌ Conjunction	0°	● New Moon (1st Quarter)
✶ Sextile	60°	◗ Waxing Moon (2nd Quarter)
☐ Square	90°	○ Full Moon (3rd Quarter)
△ Trine	120°	◑ Waning Moon (4th Quarter)
⚻ Quincunx	150°	
☍ Opposition	180°	

OCTOBER 2020

SU	M	T	W
27	28	29	30
4 3rd ♉ ♀ D 9:32 am	**5** 3rd ♉ ☽ v/c 2:41 pm	**6** 3rd ♉ ☽ → ♊ 12:03 am	**7** 3rd ♊ ☽ v/c 9:57 pm
11 4th ♌	**12** 4th ♌ ☽ v/c 10:29 am	**13** 4th ♌ ☽ → ♍ 12:56 am ☿ R 9:05 pm *Mercury retrograde*	**14** 4th ♍ ☽ v/c 6:47 pm
18 1st ♏ ☽ v/c 5:43 pm	**19** 1st ♏ ☽ → ♐ 12:43 am	**20** 1st ♐ ☽ v/c 11:38 pm	**21** 1st ♐ ☽ → ♑ 2:44 am
25 2nd ♒ ☽ → ♓ 5:18 pm	**26** 2nd ♓	**27** 2nd ♓ ☽ v/c 8:46 pm ☿ → ♎ 9:33 pm ♀ → ♎ 9:41 pm	**28** 2nd ♓ ☽ → ♈ 4:45 am
1	2	3	4

Eastern Daylight Time (EDT)

ZODIAC SIGNS

♈ Aries	♌ Leo	♐ Sagittarius
♉ Taurus	♍ Virgo	♑ Capricorn
♊ Gemini	♎ Libra	♒ Aquarius
♋ Cancer	♏ Scorpio	♓ Pisces

PLANETS

☉ Sun	♃ Jupiter
☽ Moon	♄ Saturn
☿ Mercury	♅ Uranus
♀ Venus	♆ Neptune
♂ Mars	♇ Pluto

OCTOBER 2020

TH	F	SA	NOTES
2nd ♈ ○ Full Moon 5:05 pm *Blood Moon*	3rd ♈ 2 ♀ → ♍ 4:48 pm	3rd ♈ 3 ☽ v/c 1:47 am ☽ → ♉ 11:12 am	
3rd ♊ 8 ☽ → ♋ 11:45 am	3rd ♋ ◐ 4th Quarter 8:40 pm	4th ♋ 10 ☽ v/c 12:04 pm ☽ → ♌ 8:24 pm	
4th ♍ 15 ☽ → ♎ 1:54 am	4th ♎ ● New Moon 3:31 pm ☽ v/c 6:11 pm *New Moon*	1st ♎ 17 ☽ → ♏ 1:05 am	
1st ♑ 22 ☉ → ♏ 7:00 pm *Sun enters Scorpio*	1st ♑ ◑ ☽ v/c 12:35 am ☽ → ♒ 8:17 am 2nd Quarter 9:23 am	2nd ♒ 24 ☽ v/c 5:54 pm	
2nd ♈ 29	2nd ♈ 30 ☽ v/c 12:12 pm ☽ → ♉ 5:19 pm	2nd ♉ ○ Full Moon 10:49 am *Samhain* *Halloween*	
5	6	7	

Aspects & Moon Phases

☌ Conjunction	0°	● New Moon	(1st Quarter)
✳ Sextile	60°	◐ Waxing Moon	(2nd Quarter)
☐ Square	90°	○ Full Moon	(3rd Quarter)
△ Trine	120°	◑ Waning Moon	(4th Quarter)
⊼ Quincunx	150°		
☍ Opposition	180°		

NOVEMBER 2020

SU	M	T	W
1 3rd ♉ ☽ v/c 9:29 pm *Daylight Saving Time* *ends at 2:00 am*	**2** 3rd ♉ ☽ → ♊ 5:00 am	**3** 3rd ♊ ☿ D 12:50 pm *Mercury direct* *Election Day (general)*	**4** 3rd ♊ ☽ v/c 8:49 am ☽ → ♋ 4:45 pm
8 3rd ♌ 4th Quarter 8:46 am ◑	**9** 4th ♌ ☽ v/c 6:05 am ☽ → ♍ 8:30 am	**10** 4th ♍ ☿ → ♏ 4:55 pm	**11** 4th ♍ ☽ v/c 5:58 am ☽ → ♎ 11:09 am
15 4th ♏ New Moon 12:07 am ● ☽ v/c 6:13 am ☽ → ♐ 10:47 am *New Moon*	**16** 1st ♐	**17** 1st ♐ ☽ v/c 2:55 am ☽ → ♑ 11:35 am	**18** 1st ♑
22 2nd ♓	**23** 2nd ♓	**24** 2nd ♓ ☽ v/c 5:44 am ☽ → ♈ 10:05 am	**25** 2nd ♈
29 2nd ♉ ☽ v/c 7:48 am ☽ → ♊ 11:16 am	**30** 2nd ♊ Full Moon 4:30 am ○ ☽ v/c 11:22 pm *Mourning Moon* *Lunar Eclipse*	**1**	**2**
6	**7**	**8**	**9**

Eastern Daylight Time (EDT) becomes Eastern Standard Time (EST) November 1

NOVEMBER 2020

TH	F	SA	NOTES
3rd ⊗ **5**	3rd ⊗ **6** ☽ v/c 8:27 pm	3rd ⊗ **7** ☽ → ♌ 2:18 am	
4th ♎ **12**	4th ♎ **13** ☽ v/c 6:32 am ☽ → ♏ 11:19 am ♂ D 7:36 pm *Mars direct*	4th ♏ **14**	
1st ♑ **19** ☽ v/c 11:30 am ☽ → ♒ 3:25 pm	1st ♒ **20** ☽ v/c 7:49 pm	1st ♒ **20** ◑ ♀ → ♏ 8:22 am ☉ → ♐ 3:40 pm ☽ → ♓ 11:06 pm 2nd Quarter 11:45 pm *Sun enters Sagittarius*	
2nd ♈ **26** ☽ v/c 6:46 pm ☽ → ♉ 10:43 pm *Thanksgiving Day*	2nd ♉ **27**	2nd ♉ **28** ♆ D 7:36 pm	
3	**4**	**5**	
10	**11**	**12**	

Aspects & Moon Phases

☌ Conjunction	0°	● New Moon	(1st Quarter)
✶ Sextile	60°	◐ Waxing Moon	(2nd Quarter)
☐ Square	90°	○ Full Moon	(3rd Quarter)
△ Trine	120°	◑ Waning Moon	(4th Quarter)
⚻ Quincunx	150°		
☍ Opposition	180°		

DECEMBER 2020

SU	M	T	W
29	30	**1** 3rd ♊ ☿ → ♐ 2:51 pm ☽ → ♋ 10:33 pm	**2** 3rd ♋
6 3rd ♌ ☽ → ♍ 2:46 pm	**7** 3rd ♍ 4th Quarter 7:37 pm ◐	**8** 4th ♍ ☽ v/c 5:35 pm ☽ → ♎ 7:01 pm	**9** 4th ♎
13 4th ♐	**14** 4th ♐ ☽ v/c 11:17 am New Moon 11:17 am ☽ → ♑ 10:35 pm ● *New Moon* *Solar Eclipse*	**15** 1st ♑ ♀ → ♐ 11:21 am	**16** 1st ♑
20 1st ♓ ☿ → ♑ 6:07 pm	**21** 1st ♓ ☉ → ♑ 5:02 am ☽ v/c 5:25 am ☽ → ♈ 5:32 pm 2nd Quarter 6:41 pm ◐ *Yule* *Sun enters Capricorn* *Winter Solstice*	**22** 2nd ♈	**23** 2nd ♈ ☽ v/c 5:51 pm
27 2nd ♊	**28** 2nd ♊ ☽ v/c 10:01 pm	**29** 2nd ♊ ☽ → ♋ 5:28 am Full Moon 10:28 pm ○ *Long Nights Moon*	**30** 3rd ♋
3	4	5	6

Eastern Standard Time (EST)

ZODIAC SIGNS

♈ Aries	♌ Leo	♐ Sagittarius
♉ Taurus	♍ Virgo	♑ Capricorn
♊ Gemini	♎ Libra	♒ Aquarius
♋ Cancer	♏ Scorpio	♓ Pisces

PLANETS

☉ Sun	♃ Jupiter
☽ Moon	♄ Saturn
☿ Mercury	♅ Uranus
♀ Venus	♆ Neptune
♂ Mars	♇ Pluto

DECEMBER 2020

TH	F	SA	NOTES
3rd ⊚ **3**	3rd ⊚ **4** ☽ v/c 5:29 am ☽ → ♌ 7:53 am	3rd ♌ **5** ☽ v/c 5:28 pm	
4th ♎ **10** ☽ v/c 7:56 pm ☽ → ♏ 8:59 pm	4th ♏ **11**	4th ♏ **12** ☽ v/c 8:58 pm ☽ → ♐ 9:39 pm	
1st ♑ **17** ♄ → ♒ 12:04 am ☽ v/c 12:34 am ☽ → ♒ 1:27 am	1st ♒ **18**	1st ♒ **19** ☽ v/c 3:45 am ☽ → ♓ 7:39 am ♃ → ♒ 8:07 am	
2nd ♈ **24** ☽ → ♉ 5:55 am *Christmas Eve*	2nd ♉ **25** *Christmas Day*	2nd ♉ **26** ☽ v/c 6:32 am ☽ → ♊ 6:33 pm	
3rd ⊚ **31** ☽ v/c 8:45 am ☽ → ♌ 1:58 pm *New Year's Eve*	*1*	*2*	
7	*8*	*9*	

JANUARY 2021

SU	M	T	W
27	28	29	30
3 3rd ♍	**4** 3rd ♍ ☽ v/c 4:34 pm	**5** 3rd ♍ ☽ → ♎ 12:42 am	**30 / 5** ◗ 3rd ♎ 4th Quarter 4:37 am ♂ → ♉ 5:27 pm
10 4th ♐ ☽ v/c 1:29 pm	**11** 4th ♐ ☽ → ♑ 8:30 am	**12** 4th ♑	**12** ● 4th ♑ New Moon 12:00 am ☽ v/c 2:22 am ☽ → ♒ 11:44 am *New Moon*
17 1st ♓ ☽ v/c 10:44 pm	**18** 1st ♓ ☽ → ♈ 2:07 am *Martin Luther King Jr. Day*	**19** 1st ♈ ☉ → ♒ 3:40 pm *Sun enters Aquarius*	**19** ◑ 1st ♈ ☽ v/c 3:29 pm ☽ → ♉ 1:56 pm 2nd Quarter 4:02 pm
24 2nd ♊	**25** 2nd ♊ ☽ v/c 2:17 am ☽ → ♋ 1:52 pm	**26** 2nd ♋	**27** 2nd ♋ ☽ v/c 12:55 pm ☽ → ♌ 9:54 pm
31 3rd ♍	1	2	3

Eastern Standard Time (EST)

JANUARY 2021

TH	F	SA	NOTES
31	3rd ♌︎ 1	3rd ♌︎ 2 ☽ v/c 5:00 pm ☽ → ♍︎ 8:13 pm	
	New Year's Day		
4th ♎︎ 7 ☽ v/c 12:55 am ☽ → ♏︎ 3:53 am	4th ♏︎ 8 ☿ → ♒︎ 7:00 am ♀ → ♑︎ 10:41 am ☽ v/c 8:59 pm	4th ♏︎ 9 ☽ → ♐︎ 6:15 am	
1st ♒︎ 14 ♅ D 3:36 am ☽ v/c 4:28 am	1st ♒︎ 15 ☽ → ♓︎ 5:17 pm	1st ♓︎ 16	
2nd ♉︎ 21	2nd ♉︎ 22 ☽ v/c 4:28 pm	2nd ♉︎ 23 ☽ → ♊︎ 2:43 am	
2nd ♌︎ ○ Full Moon 2:16 pm	3rd ♌︎ 29 ☽ v/c 8:53 pm	3rd ♌︎ 30 ☽ → ♍︎ 3:02 am ☿ ℞ 10:52 am	
Cold Moon		*Mercury retrograde*	
4	5	6	

Aspects & Moon Phases

☌ Conjunction	0°	● New Moon	(1st Quarter)	
✶ Sextile	60°	◐ Waxing Moon	(2nd Quarter)	
☐ Square	90°	○ Full Moon	(3rd Quarter)	
△ Trine	120°	◑ Waning Moon	(4th Quarter)	
⊼ Quincunx	150°			
☍ Opposition	180°			

FEBRUARY 2021

SU	M	T	W
31	**1** 3rd ♍ ☽ v/c 6:10 am ☽ → ♎ 6:25 am ♀ → ♒ 9:05 am	**2** 3rd ♎ *Imbolc* *Groundhog Day*	**3** 3rd ♎ ☽ v/c 1:15 am ☽ → ♏ 9:15 am
7 4th ♐ ☽ v/c 1:16 am ☽ → ♑ 3:52 pm	**8** 4th ♑	**9** 4th ♑ ☽ v/c 12:22 pm ☽ → ♒ 8:20 pm	**10** 4th ♒
14 1st ♓ ☽ v/c 2:29 am ☽ → ♈ 10:54 am *Valentine's Day*	**15** 1st ♈ *Presidents' Day*	**16** 1st ♈ ☽ v/c 7:17 pm ☽ → ♉ 10:12 pm *Mardi Gras (Fat Tuesday)*	**17** 1st ♉ *Ash Wednesday*
21 2nd ♊ ☽ v/c 1:39 pm ☽ → ♋ 10:53 pm	**22** 2nd ♋	**23** 2nd ♋ ☽ v/c 11:54 pm	**24** 2nd ♋ ☽ → ♌ 7:23 am
28 3rd ♍ ☽ v/c 10:58 am ☽ → ♎ 2:17 pm	**1**	**2**	**3**
7	**8**	**9**	**10**

Eastern Standard Time (EST)

♈ Aries ♌ Leo ♐ Sagittarius
♉ Taurus ♍ Virgo ♑ Capricorn
♊ Gemini ♎ Libra ♒ Aquarius
♋ Cancer ♏ Scorpio ♓ Pisces

PLANETS

☉ Sun ♃ Jupiter
☽ Moon ♄ Saturn
☿ Mercury ♅ Uranus
♀ Venus ♆ Neptune
♂ Mars ♇ Pluto

FEBRUARY 2021

TH	F	SA	NOTES
3rd ♏ 4th Quarter 12:37 pm ◑	4th ♏ **5** ☽ v/c 4:20 am ☽ → ♐ 12:16 pm	4th ♐ **6**	
4th ♒ ● ☽ v/c 2:06 pm New Moon 2:06 pm *New Moon*	1st ♒ **12** ☽ → ♓ 2:23 am *Lunar New Year (Ox)*	1st ♓ **13**	
1st ♉ **18** ☉ → ♓ 5:44 am *Sun enters Pisces*	1st ♉ ◑ ☽ v/c 2:28 am ☽ → ♊ 11:04 am 2nd Quarter 1:47 pm	2nd ♊ **20** ☿ D 7:52 pm *Mercury direct*	
2nd ♌ **25** ♀ → ♓ 8:11 am	2nd ♌ **26** ☽ v/c 6:32 am ☽ → ♍ 12:07 pm *Quickening Moon*	2nd ♍ ○ Full Moon 3:17 am	
4	**5**	**6**	
11	**12**	**13**	

ASPECTS & MOON PHASES

☌ Conjunction	0°	● New Moon	(1st Quarter)
✶ Sextile	60°	◗ Waxing Moon	(2nd Quarter)
☐ Square	90°	○ Full Moon	(3rd Quarter)
△ Trine	120°	◖ Waning Moon	(4th Quarter)
⚻ Quincunx	150°		
☍ Opposition	180°		

MARCH 2021

SU	M	T	W
28	3rd ♎ **1**	3rd ♎ ☽ v/c 9:09 am ☽ → ♏ 3:38 pm **2**	3rd ♏ ♂ → ♊ 10:30 pm **3**
4th ♑ **7**	4th ♑ ☽ v/c 7:52 pm **8**	4th ♑ ☽ → ♒ 2:41 am **9**	4th ♒ ☽ v/c 10:32 pm **10**
1st ♈ **14** *Daylight Saving Time begins at 2:00 am*	1st ♈ ☿ → ♓ 6:26 pm ☽ v/c 11:40 pm **15**	1st ♈ ☽ → ♉ 6:56 am **16**	1st ♉ **17** *St. Patrick's Day*
1st ♊ ◑ ☽ v/c 8:04 am ☽ → ♋ 8:18 am ♀ → ♈ 10:16 am 2nd Quarter 10:40 am	2nd ♋ **22**	2nd ♋ ☽ v/c 11:26 am ☽ → ♌ 5:56 pm **23**	2nd ♌ **24**
2nd ♍ ○ ☽ → ♎ 1:22 am Full Moon 2:48 pm *Storm Moon*	3rd ♎ ☽ v/c 8:08 pm **29**	3rd ♎ ☽ → ♏ 1:33 am **30**	3rd ♏ ☽ v/c 8:29 pm **31**
4	5	6	7

Eastern Standard Time (EST) becomes Eastern Daylight Time (EDT) March 14

ZODIAC SIGNS

♈ Aries	♌ Leo	♐ Sagittarius
♉ Taurus	♍ Virgo	♑ Capricorn
♊ Gemini	♎ Libra	♒ Aquarius
♋ Cancer	♏ Scorpio	♓ Pisces

PLANETS

☉ Sun	♃ Jupiter
☽ Moon	♄ Saturn
☿ Mercury	♅ Uranus
♀ Venus	♆ Neptune
♂ Mars	♇ Pluto

MARCH 2021

TH	F	SA	NOTES
3rd ♏ **4** ☽ v/c 11:10 am ☽ → ♐ 5:43 pm	3rd ♐ ◑ 4th Quarter 8:30 pm	4th ♐ **6** ☽ v/c 4:44 am ☽ → ♑ 9:20 pm	
4th ♒ **11** ☽ → ♓ 9:44 am	4th ♓ **12**	4th ♓ ● New Moon 5:21 am ☽ v/c 11:38 am ☽ → ♈ 6:44 pm *New Moon*	
1st ♉ **18** ☽ v/c 4:40 pm ☽ → ♊ 7:47 pm	1st ♊ **19**	1st ♊ **20** ☉ → ♈ 5:37 am *Ostara* *Sun enters Aries* *Spring Equinox*	
2nd ♌ **25** ☽ v/c 9:27 am ☽ → ♍ 11:25 pm	2nd ♍ **26**	2nd ♍ **27** ☽ v/c 7:48 pm	
1	2	3	
8	9	10	

ASPECTS & MOON PHASES

☌ Conjunction	0°	● New Moon	(1st Quarter)
⚹ Sextile	60°	◐ Waxing Moon	(2nd Quarter)
☐ Square	90°	○ Full Moon	(3rd Quarter)
△ Trine	120°	◑ Waning Moon	(4th Quarter)
⚻ Quincunx	150°		
☍ Opposition	180°		

APRIL 2021

SU	M	T	W
28	29	30	31
3rd ♈︎ ◑ 4th Quarter 6:02 am *Easter*	4th ♑ 5 ☽ v/c 3:05 am ☽ → ♒ 9:04 am	4th ♒ 6	4th ♒ 7 ☽ v/c 6:05 am ☽ → ♓ 4:30 pm
4th ♈︎ ● New Moon 10:31 pm *New Moon*	1st ♈︎ 12 ☽ v/c 8:06 am ☽ → ♉ 1:44 pm	1st ♉ 13	1st ♉ 14 ♀ → ♉ 2:22 pm ☽ v/c 8:00 pm
1st ♋ 18	1st ♋ 19 ☿ → ♉ 6:29 am ☉ → ♉ 4:33 pm ☽ v/c 8:03 pm *Sun enters Taurus*	1st ♋ ◐ ☽ → ♌ 2:11 am 2nd Quarter 2:59 am	2nd ♌ 21
2nd ♎ 25	2nd ♎ ○ ☽ v/c 8:40 am ☽ → ♏ 12:18 pm Full Moon 11:32 pm *Wind Moon*	3rd ♏ 27 ♀ ℞ 4:04 pm	3rd ♏ 28 ☽ v/c 8:31 am ☽ → ♐ 11:42 am
2	3	4	5

Eastern Daylight Time (EDT)

ZODIAC SIGNS

♈︎ Aries	♌ Leo	♐ Sagittarius
♉ Taurus	♍ Virgo	♑ Capricorn
♊ Gemini	♎ Libra	♒ Aquarius
♋ Cancer	♏ Scorpio	♓ Pisces

PLANETS

☉ Sun	♃ Jupiter
☽ Moon	♄ Saturn
☿ Mercury	♅ Uranus
♀ Venus	♆ Neptune
♂ Mars	♇ Pluto

APRIL 2021

TH		F		SA		NOTES
3rd ♏︎ ☽ → ♐︎ 1:59 am *All Fools' Day*	**1**	3rd ♐︎	**2**	3rd ♐︎ ☽ v/c 1:24 am ☽ → ♑︎ 4:13 am ☿ → ♈︎ 11:41 pm	**3**	
4th ♓︎	**8**	4th ♓︎ ☽ v/c 7:48 pm	**9**	4th ♓︎ ☽ → ♈︎ 2:11 am	**10**	
1st ♉︎ ☽ → ♊︎ 2:35 am	**15**	1st ♊︎	**16**	1st ♊︎ ☽ v/c 11:03 am ☽ → ♋︎ 3:25 pm	**17**	
2nd ♌︎ ☽ v/c 8:05 am ☽ → ♍︎ 9:08 am *Earth Day*	**22**	2nd ♍︎ ♂ → ♋︎ 7:49 am	**23**	2nd ♍︎ ☽ v/c 6:50 am ☽ → ♎︎ 12:06 pm	**24**	
3rd ♐︎	**29**	3rd ♐︎ ☽ v/c 9:27 am ☽ → ♑︎ 12:16 pm	**30**		*1*	
	6		*7*		*8*	

ASPECTS & MOON PHASES

☌ Conjunction	0°	● New Moon	(1st Quarter)		
⚹ Sextile	60°	◐ Waxing Moon	(2nd Quarter)		
☐ Square	90°	○ Full Moon	(3rd Quarter)		
△ Trine	120°	◑ Waning Moon	(4th Quarter)		
⚻ Quincunx	150°				
☍ Opposition	180°				

MAY 2021

SU	M	T	W
25	26	27	28
2 3rd ♑ ☽ v/c 10:38 am ☽ → ♒ 3:31 pm	**3** ◑ 3rd ♒ 4th Quarter 3:50 pm ☿ → ♊ 10:49 pm	**4** 4th ♒ ☽ v/c 8:05 pm ☽ → ♓ 10:09 pm	**5** 4th ♓
9 4th ♈ ☽ v/c 6:50 pm ☽ → ♉ 7:46 pm *Mother's Day*	**10** 4th ♉	**11** ● 4th ♉ New Moon 3:00 pm *New Moon*	**12** 1st ♉ ☽ v/c 8:23 am ☽ → ♊ 8:43 am
16 1st ♋	**17** 1st ♋ ☽ v/c 2:23 am ☽ → ♌ 8:44 am	**18** 1st ♌	**19** ◑ 1st ♌ ☽ v/c 3:13 pm 2nd Quarter 3:13 pm ☽ → ♍ 4:59 pm
23 2nd ♎ ♄ ℞ 5:21 am ☽ v/c 5:36 pm ☽ → ♏ 11:00 pm	**24** 2nd ♏	**25** 2nd ♏ ☽ v/c 5:20 pm ☽ → ♐ 10:39 pm	**25** ○ 2nd ♐ Full Moon 7:14 am *Flower Moon* *Lunar Eclipse*
30 3rd ♑ ☽ → ♒ 12:04 am	**31** 3rd ♒ *Memorial Day*	**1** ♊	**2**

Eastern Daylight Time (EDT)

ZODIAC SIGNS

♈ Aries	♌ Leo	♐ Sagittarius
♉ Taurus	♍ Virgo	♑ Capricorn
♊ Gemini	♎ Libra	♒ Aquarius
♋ Cancer	♏ Scorpio	♓ Pisces

PLANETS

☉ Sun	♃ Jupiter
☽ Moon	♄ Saturn
☿ Mercury	♅ Uranus
♀ Venus	♆ Neptune
♂ Mars	♇ Pluto

TH	F	SA	NOTES
29	30	3rd ♑ 1 *Beltane*	
4th ♓ 6	4th ♓ 7 ☽ v/c 3:36 am ☽ → ♈ 7:52 am	4th ♈ 8 ♀ → ♊ 10:01 pm	
1st ♊ 13 ♃ → ♓ 6:36 pm	1st ♊ 14 ☽ v/c 6:51 am ☽ → ♋ 9:30 pm	1st ♋ 15	
2nd ♍ 20 ☉ → ♊ 3:37 pm *Sun enters Gemini*	2nd ♍ 21 ☽ v/c 3:56 pm ☽ → ♎ 9:35 pm	2nd ♎ 22	
3rd ♐ 27 ☽ v/c 1:35 pm ☽ → ♑ 10:23 pm	3rd ♑ 28	3rd ♑ 29 ☽ v/c 6:15 pm ☿ Ŗ 6:34 pm *Mercury retrograde*	
3	4	5	

ASPECTS & MOON PHASES

☌ Conjunction	0°	● New Moon	(1st Quarter)	
✶ Sextile	60°	◗ Waxing Moon	(2nd Quarter)	
□ Square	90°	○ Full Moon	(3rd Quarter)	
△ Trine	120°	◐ Waning Moon	(4th Quarter)	
⊼ Quincunx	150°			
☍ Opposition	180°			

JUNE 2021

SU	M	T	W
30	31	3rd ≈≈ 1 ☽ v/c 2:14 am ☽ → ♓ 5:07 am	3rd ♓ 4th Quarter 3:24 am ♀ → ♋ 9:19 am ◑
6 4th ♈ ☽ → ♉ 1:46 am	7 4th ♉	8 4th ♉ ☽ v/c 11:07 am ☽ → ♊ 2:47 pm	9 4th ♊
13 1st ♋ ☽ v/c 7:16 am ☽ → ♌ 2:22 pm	14 1st ♌	15 1st ♌ ☽ v/c 1:27 pm ☽ → ♍ 11:02 pm	16 1st ♍
20 2nd ♎ ☽ v/c 6:52 am ☽ → ♏ 7:58 am ♃ ℞ 11:06 am ⊙ → ♋ 11:32 pm *Father's Day/Litha* *Sun enters Cancer* *Summer Solstice*	21 2nd ♏	22 2nd ♏ ☽ v/c 2:43 am ☽ → ♐ 8:55 am ☿ D 6:00 pm *Mercury direct*	23 2nd ♐ ☽ v/c 10:09 pm
27 3rd ≈≈ ♀ → ♌ 12:27 am ☽ v/c 3:08 pm	28 3rd ≈≈ ☽ → ♓ 1:51 pm	29 3rd ♓	30 3rd ♓ ☽ v/c 1:40 pm ☽ → ♈ 9:21 pm
4	5	6	7

Eastern Daylight Time (EDT)

ZODIAC SIGNS

♈ Aries	♌ Leo	♐ Sagittarius
♉ Taurus	♍ Virgo	♑ Capricorn
♊ Gemini	♎ Libra	≈≈ Aquarius
♋ Cancer	♏ Scorpio	♓ Pisces

PLANETS

⊙ Sun	♃ Jupiter
☽ Moon	♄ Saturn
☿ Mercury	♅ Uranus
♀ Venus	♆ Neptune
♂ Mars	♇ Pluto

JUNE 2021

TH	F	SA	NOTES
3 4th ♓ ☽ v/c 7:10 am ☽ → ♈ 1:59 pm	**4** 4th ♈	**5** 4th ♈ ☽ v/c 6:47 pm	
10 4th ♊ New Moon 6:53 am ☽ v/c 1:38 pm *New Moon* *Solar Eclipse* ●	**11** 1st ♊ ☽ → ♋ 3:23 am ♂ → ♌ 9:34 am	**12** 1st ♋	
17 1st ♍ ☽ v/c 11:54 pm 2nd Quarter 11:54 pm ◑	**18** 2nd ♍ ☽ → ♎ 4:54 am	**19** 2nd ♎	
24 2nd ♐ ☽ → ♑ 9:05 am Full Moon 2:40 pm *Strong Sun Moon* ○	**25** 3rd ♑ Ψ ℞ 3:21 pm	**26** 3rd ♑ ☽ v/c 8:49 am ☽ → ♒ 10:09 am	
1	2	3	
8	9	10	

ASPECTS & MOON PHASES

☌ Conjunction	0°	● New Moon	(1st Quarter)
⚹ Sextile	60°	◐ Waxing Moon	(2nd Quarter)
☐ Square	90°	○ Full Moon	(3rd Quarter)
△ Trine	120°	◑ Waning Moon	(4th Quarter)
⚻ Quincunx	150°		
☍ Opposition	180°		

JULY 2021

SU	M	T	W
27	28	29	30
4 4th ♉	**5** 4th ♉ ☽ v/c 12:57 pm ☽ → ♊ 9:24 pm	**6** 4th ♊	**7** 4th ♊
Independence Day			
11 1st ♌ ☿ → ♋ 4:35 pm	**12** 1st ♌ ☽ v/c 8:29 am	**13** 1st ♌ ☽ → ♍ 4:30 am	**14** 1st ♍
18 2nd ♏	**19** 2nd ♏ ☽ v/c 12:30 pm ☽ → ♐ 5:08 pm	**20** 2nd ♐	**21** 2nd ♐ ☽ v/c 6:26 pm ☽ → ♑ 6:36 pm ♀ → ♍ 8:37 pm
25 3rd ♒ ☽ v/c 7:14 pm ☽ → ♓ 11:30 pm	**26** 3rd ♓	**27** 3rd ♓ ☿ → ♌ 9:12 pm ☽ v/c 9:13 pm	**28** 3rd ♓ ☽ → ♈ 5:58 am ♃ → ♒ 8:43 am
1	2	3	4

Eastern Daylight Time (EDT)

ZODIAC SIGNS

♈ Aries ♌ Leo ♐ Sagittarius
♉ Taurus ♍ Virgo ♑ Capricorn
♊ Gemini ♎ Libra ♒ Aquarius
♋ Cancer ♏ Scorpio ♓ Pisces

PLANETS

☉ Sun ♃ Jupiter
☽ Moon ♄ Saturn
☿ Mercury ♅ Uranus
♀ Venus ♆ Neptune
♂ Mars ♇ Pluto

TH	F	SA	NOTES
3rd ♈ ◑ 4th Quarter 5:11 pm	4th ♈ **I**	4th ♈ **3** ☽ v/c 12:15 am ☽ → ♉ 8:28 am	
4th ♊ **8** ☽ v/c 12:20 am ☽ → ♋ 9:51 am	4th ♋ ● New Moon 9:17 pm *New Moon*	1st ♋ **10** ☽ v/c 12:10 pm ☽ → ♌ 8:21 pm	
1st ♍ **15** ☽ v/c 2:46 am ☽ → ♎ 10:32 am	1st ♎ **16**	1st ♎ ◑ 2nd Quarter 6:11 am ☽ v/c 7:03 am ☽ → ♏ 2:38 pm	
2nd ♑ **22** ☉ → ♌ 10:26 am *Sun enters Leo*	2nd ♑ ○ ☽ v/c 12:34 pm ☽ → ♒ 8:12 pm Full Moon 10:37 pm *Blessing Moon*	3rd ♒ **24**	
3rd ♈ **29** ♂ → ♍ 4:32 pm	3rd ♈ **30** ☽ v/c 3:38 pm ☽ → ♉ 4:08 pm	3rd ♉ ◑ 4th Quarter 9:16 am	
5	*6*	*7*	

AUGUST 2021

SU	M	T	W
1 4th ♉ *Lammas*	**2** 4th ♉ ☽ v/c 3:41 am ☽ → ♊ 4:46 am	**3** 4th ♊	**4** 4th ♊ ☽ v/c 3:38 pm ☽ → ♋ 5:17 pm
4th ♌ New Moon 9:50 am ● *New Moon*	**9** 1st ♌ ☽ v/c 8:23 am ☽ → ♍ 10:56 am	**10** 1st ♍	**11** 1st ♍ ☽ v/c 7:22 am ☽ → ♎ 4:08 pm ☿ → ♍ 5:57 pm
1st ♏ ◑ 2nd Quarter 11:20 am ☽ v/c 11:05 pm ☽ → ♐ 11:12 pm	**16** 2nd ♐ ♀ → ♎ 12:27 am	**17** 2nd ♐ ☽ v/c 9:43 pm	**18** 2nd ♐ ☽ → ♑ 1:58 am
2nd ♒ ○ ☽ v/c 8:02 am Full Moon 8:02 am ☽ → ♓ 8:43 am ☉ → ♍ 5:35 pm *Corn Moon* *Sun enters Virgo*	**23** 3rd ♓	**24** 3rd ♓ ☽ v/c 5:12 am ☽ → ♈ 2:57 pm	**25** 3rd ♈
29 3rd ♉ ☽ v/c 10:59 am ☽ → ♊ 12:42 pm	**30** 3rd ♊ ◐ ☿ → ♎ 1:10 am 4th Quarter 3:13 am	**31** 4th ♊ ☽ v/c 4:48 pm	**1**
5	**6**	**7**	**8**

Eastern Daylight Time (EDT)

ZODIAC SIGNS

♈ Aries	♌ Leo	♐ Sagittarius
♉ Taurus	♍ Virgo	♑ Capricorn
♊ Gemini	♎ Libra	♒ Aquarius
♋ Cancer	♏ Scorpio	♓ Pisces

PLANETS

☉ Sun	♃ Jupiter
☽ Moon	♄ Saturn
☿ Mercury	♅ Uranus
♀ Venus	♆ Neptune
♂ Mars	♇ Pluto

AUGUST 2021

TH	F	SA	NOTES
4th ♋ **5**	4th ♋ **6** ☽ v/c 6:12 pm	4th ♋ **7** ☽ → ♌ 3:31 am	
1st ♎ **12**	1st ♎ **13** ☽ v/c 4:39 pm ☽ → ♏ 8:01 pm	1st ♏ **14**	
2nd ♑ **19** ☽ v/c 7:59 pm ♅ ℞ 9:40 pm	2nd ♑ **20** ☽ → ♒ 4:49 am	2nd ♒ **21**	
3rd ♈ **26** ☽ v/c 5:14 pm	3rd ♈ **27** ☽ → ♉ 12:27 am	3rd ♉ **28**	
2	**3**	**4**	
9	**10**	**11**	

Aspects & Moon Phases

☌ Conjunction	0°	● New Moon	(1st Quarter)
✶ Sextile	60°	◗ Waxing Moon	(2nd Quarter)
☐ Square	90°	○ Full Moon	(3rd Quarter)
△ Trine	120°	◖ Waning Moon	(4th Quarter)
⊼ Quincunx	150°		
☍ Opposition	180°		

SEPTEMBER 2021

SU	M	T	W
29	30	31	**1** 4th ♊ ☽ → ♋ 1:26 am
5 4th ♌ ☽ v/c 10:22 am ☽ → ♍ 7:06 pm	**30 / 6** 4th ♍ New Moon 8:52 pm ● *New Moon* *Labor Day*	**7** 1st ♍ ☽ v/c 3:24 pm ☽ → ♎ 11:20 pm	**8** 1st ♎
12 1st ♏ ☽ v/c 1:33 am ☽ → ♐ 4:34 am	**13** 1st ♐ 2nd Quarter 4:39 pm ◗	**14** 2nd ♐ ☽ v/c 6:57 am ☽ → ♑ 7:34 am ♂ → ♎ 8:14 pm	**15** 2nd ♑
19 2nd ♓	**20** 2nd ♓ ☽ v/c 7:55 pm Full Moon 7:55 pm ○ ☽ → ♈ 11:13 pm *Harvest Moon*	**21** 3rd ♈	**22** 3rd ♈ ☉ → ♎ 3:21 pm ☽ v/c 10:05 pm *Mabon* *Sun enters Libra* *Fall Equinox*
26 3rd ♊	**27** 3rd ♊ ☿ ℞ 1:10 am *Mercury retrograde*	**28** 3rd ♊ ☽ v/c 12:18 am ☽ → ♋ 9:34 am 4th Quarter 9:57 pm ◑	**29** 4th ♋
3	4	5	6

Eastern Daylight Time (EDT)

ZODIAC SIGNS

♈ Aries	♌ Leo	♐ Sagittarius
♉ Taurus	♍ Virgo	♑ Capricorn
♊ Gemini	♎ Libra	♒ Aquarius
♋ Cancer	♏ Scorpio	♓ Pisces

PLANETS

☉ Sun	♃ Jupiter
☽ Moon	♄ Saturn
☿ Mercury	♅ Uranus
♀ Venus	♆ Neptune
♂ Mars	♇ Pluto

SEPTEMBER 2021

TH	F	SA	NOTES
4th ⊗ **2**	4th ⊗ **3** ☽ v/c 1:37 am ☽ → ♌ 11:58 am	4th ♌ **4**	
1st ♎ **9**	1st ♎ **10** ☽ v/c 12:48 am ☽ → ♏ 2:05 am ♀ → ♏ 4:39 pm	1st ♏ **11**	
2nd ♑ **16** ☽ v/c 1:40 am ☽ → ♒ 11:23 am	2nd ♒ **17**	2nd ♒ **18** ☽ v/c 5:14 am ☽ → ♓ 4:22 pm	
3rd ♈ **23** ☽ → ♉ 8:38 am	3rd ♉ **24**	3rd ♉ **25** ☽ v/c 9:09 am ☽ → ♊ 8:36 pm	
4th ⊗ **30** ☽ v/c 10:49 am ☽ → ♌ 8:53 pm	*1*	*2*	
7	*8*	*9*	

ASPECTS & MOON PHASES

☌ Conjunction	0°	● New Moon	(1st Quarter)
✷ Sextile	60°	◗ Waxing Moon	(2nd Quarter)
☐ Square	90°	○ Full Moon	(3rd Quarter)
△ Trine	120°	◖ Waning Moon	(4th Quarter)
⚻ Quincunx	150°		
☍ Opposition	180°		

OCTOBER 2021

SU	M	T	W
26	27	28	29
3 4th ♌ ☽ → ♍ 4:38 am	**4** 4th ♍	**5** 4th ♍ ☽ v/c 4:46 am ☽ → ♎ 8:41 am	4th ♎ ● New Moon 7:05 am ♀ D 2:29 pm *New Moon*
10 1st ♐ ♄ D 10:17 pm	**11** 1st ♐ ☽ v/c 12:30 am ☽ → ♑ 1:15 pm	**12** 1st ♑ ◑ 2nd Quarter 11:25 pm	**13** 2nd ♑ ☽ v/c 6:53 am ☽ → ♒ 4:47 pm
17 2nd ♓ ☽ v/c 7:24 pm	**18** 2nd ♓ ♃ D 1:30 am ☽ → ♈ 6:04 am ☿ D 11:17 am *Mercury direct*	**19** 2nd ♈	2nd ♈ ○ ☽ v/c 10:57 am Full Moon 10:57 am ☽ → ♉ 3:59 pm *Blood Moon*
24 3rd ♊	**25** 3rd ♊ ☽ v/c 10:11 am ☽ → ♋ 5:00 pm	**26** 3rd ♋	**27** 3rd ♋
31 4th ♍ *Samhain Halloween*	1	2	3

Eastern Daylight Time (EDT)

ZODIAC SIGNS

♈ Aries	♌ Leo	♐ Sagittarius
♉ Taurus	♍ Virgo	♑ Capricorn
♊ Gemini	♎ Libra	♒ Aquarius
♋ Cancer	♏ Scorpio	♓ Pisces

PLANETS

☉ Sun	♃ Jupiter
☽ Moon	♄ Saturn
☿ Mercury	♅ Uranus
♀ Venus	♆ Neptune
♂ Mars	♇ Pluto

OCTOBER 2021

TH	F	SA	NOTES
30	1 4th ♌	2 4th ♌ ☽ v/c 7:43 pm	
7 1st ♎ ☽ v/c 1:03 am ♀ → ♐ 7:21 am ☽ → ♏ 10:22 am	8 1st ♏	9 1st ♏ ☽ v/c 2:05 am ☽ → ♐ 11:24 am	
14 2nd ♒	15 2nd ♒ ☽ v/c 8:33 am ☽ → ♓ 10:22 pm	16 2nd ♓	
21 3rd ♉	22 3rd ♉ ☽ v/c 4:35 pm	23 3rd ♉ ☉ → ♏ 12:51 am ☽ → ♊ 3:57 am *Sun enters Scorpio*	
28 ◑ 3rd ♋ ☽ v/c 2:02 am ☽ → ♌ 5:07 am 4th Quarter 4:05 pm	29 4th ♌	30 4th ♌ ☽ v/c 3:05 am ♂ → ♏ 10:21 am ☽ → ♍ 2:09 pm	
4	5	6	

NOVEMBER 2021

SU	M	T	W
31	**1** 4th ♍ ☽ v/c 1:00 pm ☽ → ♎ 7:11 pm	**2** 4th ♎	**3** 4th ♎ ☽ v/c 6:32 pm ☽ → ♏ 8:52 pm
		Election Day (general)	
7 1st ♐ ☽ v/c 8:44 am ☽ → ♑ 8:03 pm	**8** 1st ♑	**9** 1st ♑ ☽ v/c 12:51 pm ☽ → ♒ 10:03 pm	**10** 1st ♒
Daylight Saving Time ends at 2:00 am			
14 2nd ♓ ☽ v/c 12:40 am ☽ → ♈ 10:48 am	**15** 2nd ♈	**16** 2nd ♈ ☽ v/c 10:51 am ☽ → ♉ 9:18 pm	**17** 2nd ♉
21 3rd ♊ ☽ v/c 10:52 am ☉ → ♐ 9:34 pm ☽ → ♋ 10:33 pm	**22** 3rd ♋	**23** 3rd ♋	**24** 3rd ♋ ☽ v/c 12:46 am ☿ → ♐ 10:36 am ☽ → ♌ 10:59 am
Sun enters Sagittarius			
28 4th ♍ ☽ v/c 7:02 pm	**29** 4th ♍ ☽ → ♎ 3:55 am	**30** 4th ♎ ☽ v/c 11:20 pm	**1**
5	**6**	**7**	**8**

Eastern Daylight Time (EDT) becomes Eastern Standard Time (EST) November 7

ZODIAC SIGNS

♈ Aries	♌ Leo	♐ Sagittarius
♉ Taurus	♍ Virgo	♑ Capricorn
♊ Gemini	♎ Libra	♒ Aquarius
♋ Cancer	♏ Scorpio	♓ Pisces

PLANETS

☉ Sun	♃ Jupiter
☽ Moon	♄ Saturn
☿ Mercury	♅ Uranus
♀ Venus	♆ Neptune
♂ Mars	♇ Pluto

NOVEMBER 2021

TH	F	SA	NOTES
4th ♏︎ New Moon 5:15 pm ●	1st ♏︎ **5** ♀ → ♑ 6:44 am ☽ v/c 12:10 pm ☿ → ♏︎ 6:35 pm ☽ → ♐ 8:52 pm	1st ♐ **6**	
New Moon			
1st ♒ 2nd Quarter 7:46 am ◑ ☽ v/c 2:52 pm	2nd ♒ **12** ☽ → ♓ 2:54 am	2nd ♓ **13**	
2nd ♉ **18**	2nd ♉ ○ ☽ v/c 3:57 am Full Moon 3:57 am ☽ → ♊ 9:33 am *Mourning Moon* *Lunar Eclipse*	3rd ♊ **20**	
3rd ♌ **25**	3rd ♌ **26** ☽ v/c 11:24 am ☽ → ♍ 9:12 pm	3rd ♍ ◑ 4th Quarter 7:28 am	
Thanksgiving Day			
2	**3**	**4**	
9	**10**	**11**	

ASPECTS & MOON PHASES

☌ Conjunction	0°	● New Moon	(1st Quarter)
✶ Sextile	60°	◑ Waxing Moon	(2nd Quarter)
☐ Square	90°	○ Full Moon	(3rd Quarter)
△ Trine	120°	◐ Waning Moon	(4th Quarter)
⚲ Quincunx	150°		
☍ Opposition	180°		

DECEMBER 2021

SU	M	T	W
28	29	30	**1** 4th ♎︎ ☽ → ♏︎ 6:55 am Ψ D 8:22 am
5 1st ♐︎ ☽ v/c 12:08 am ☽ → ♑︎ 6:31 am	**6** 1st ♑︎ ☽ v/c 11:42 pm	**7** 1st ♑︎ ☽ → ♒︎ 6:49 am	**8** 1st ♒︎
12 2nd ♈︎	**13** 2nd ♈︎ ♂ → ♐︎ 4:53 am ☿ → ♑︎ 12:52 pm ☽ v/c 9:52 pm	**14** 2nd ♈︎ ☽ → ♉︎ 3:11 am	**15** 2nd ♉︎
19 3rd ♊︎ ☽ v/c 1:02 am ☽ → ♋︎ 4:42 am ♀ ℞ 5:36 am	**20** 3rd ♋︎	**21** 3rd ♋︎ ☽ v/c 9:44 am ☉ → ♑︎ 10:59 am ☽ → ♌︎ 4:54 am *Yule* *Sun enters Capricorn* *Winter Solstice*	**22** 3rd ♌︎
26 3rd ♍︎ ◑ ☽ v/c 3:39 am ☽ → ♎︎ 11:24 am 4th Quarter 9:24 pm	**27** 4th ♎︎	**28** 4th ♎︎ ☽ v/c 4:11 pm ☽ → ♏︎ 4:16 pm ♃ → ♓︎ 11:09 pm	**29** 4th ♏︎
2	3	4	5

Eastern Standard Time (EST)

ZODIAC SIGNS

♈︎ Aries	♌︎ Leo	♐︎ Sagittarius
♉︎ Taurus	♍︎ Virgo	♑︎ Capricorn
♊︎ Gemini	♎︎ Libra	♒︎ Aquarius
♋︎ Cancer	♏︎ Scorpio	♓︎ Pisces

PLANETS

☉ Sun	♃ Jupiter
☽ Moon	♄ Saturn
☿ Mercury	♅ Uranus
♀ Venus	Ψ Neptune
♂ Mars	♇ Pluto

DECEMBER 2021

TH	F	SA	NOTES
4th ♏︎ **2**	4th ♏︎ **3** ☽ v/c 12:22 am ☽ → ♐ 7:13 am	4th ♐ New Moon 2:43 am ● *New Moon* *Solar Eclipse*	
1st ♒ **9** ☽ v/c 5:00 am ☽ → ♓ 9:53 am	1st ♓ ◑ 2nd Quarter 8:36 pm	2nd ♓ **11** ☽ v/c 2:40 pm ☽ → ♈ 4:46 pm	
2nd ♉ **16** ☽ v/c 11:08 am ☽ → ♊ 3:43 pm	2nd ♊ **17**	2nd ♊ **18** ○ Full Moon 11:36 pm *Long Nights Moon*	
3rd ♌ **23**	3rd ♌ **24** ☽ v/c 1:39 am ☽ → ♍ 3:24 am *Christmas Eve*	3rd ♍ **25** *Christmas Day*	
4th ♏︎ **30** ☽ v/c 12:10 pm ☽ → ♐ 6:08 pm	4th ♐ **31** *New Year's Eve*	*1*	
6	*7*	*8*	

ASPECTS & MOON PHASES

☌ Conjunction	0°	● New Moon	(1st Quarter)
✶ Sextile	60°	◐ Waxing Moon	(2nd Quarter)
☐ Square	90°	○ Full Moon	(3rd Quarter)
△ Trine	120°	◑ Waning Moon	(4th Quarter)
⚻ Quincunx	150°		
☍ Opposition	180°		